BOERNE
A Brief History

Second Edition.
First edition titled "Boerne, Settlement on the Cibolo."

Copyright © 2014 by Jefferson Morgenthaler.

ISBN 9781932801309

Mockingbird Books
Boerne, Texas 78006
www.mockingbirdbooks.com

First Edition: October 2005
Second Edition: October 2014

BOERNE
A Brief History

Jefferson Morgenthaler

Mockingbird Books

For Nutty Brown, Wonder Dog

The onion dome on the Boerne bandstand is not historic. It was purchased and installed by the Boerne Optimist Club in the late 1980s. And it is not especially German—onion domes are found most often in Eastern European, Russian and Islamic architecture. For that matter, an onion dome is not even a dome, because it is not vaulted. But it is handsome and has quickly become a Boerne icon.

Table of Contents

Introduction 1
Prologue 3
Maps 9
Hill Country 13
Germans 21
Founding 27
Germania 35
Photographs 39
Hardships 69
Kendall County 75
Civil War 79
Arrivals 85
Later Years 95
Epilogue 101
Acknowledgments 105
Selected Bibliography 107
Image Credits 111

Introduction

Boerne has no grand claim to fame, but it is something that is becoming rare: a traditional American small town. It is in a beautiful setting. It has interesting history and a distinguished German heritage.

Boerne is in the early stages of explosive growth and change. A lot of good will come: jobs, schools, hospitals, commerce and amenities. And there will be changes that are not quite as welcome. This is a good time to take a look at what has gone before. Understanding Boerne's past helps us decide how we should manage and guide its future.

When writing a local history, it is tempting to open your research file and dump everything into the printing press wholesale. This approach makes friends, because everybody's Aunt Bertha ends up being mentioned somewhere in the book. But the result is more a reference manual than a history, and the story can get lost among all the family trees.

Because I did not grow up in Boerne, it may have been easier for me to take a step back and decide what should be included and what should be left out. In making those decisions I have not addressed which citizens have been most important (trust me, your Aunt Bertha was *very* important). Instead, I have looked for characters with compelling stories that move the chronicle forward. I have avoided including information just to get it on the record.

This is a history for readers. It is for visitors and newcomers and old-timers. It is for people who love Boerne, as I do.

Prologue

When we moved to Boerne more than a decade ago, we bought a seriously dilapidated property. From the road, we could see only an expanse of weeds and mud, crossed by runs of rusty, tangled barbed wire. That, and a tiny, pink-asbestos-shingled farmhouse.

The real estate agent arrived and unlocked the gate. We drove cautiously down the rutted gravel road into the barnyard. The corrugated steel doors of a low, stone dairy barn flapped in the wind. In the shadow of an old windmill, a few disreputable sheds and a rusty-roofed log barn deteriorated before our eyes.

The farmhouse's last resident, ninety-two-year-old Lottie Kohls, had died a couple of years earlier. Since then, a neighbor had been leasing the pastures to grow Sudan sorghum and had let the rest of the place go. Sudan is an annual crop used for winter feed. It was October, the crop was in and the fields were little more than mud and stubble. Gray clouds hung low and an edgy wind whistled through the oaks. Winter was coming.

Lottie's farmhouse was a tear-down. Heated (if you can call it that) by a kerosene furnace, it depended on an unreliable sixty-year-old well for water. Its interior was paneled entirely in thin sheets of plywood painted 1940s-hospital-room green.

Once we became the proud owners of Lottie's farm, we set about tidying things up. Much of this work involved a front-end loader, for Lottie and her late husband Herbert had accumulated a world-class collection of detritus. In fairness to Lottie—and we are fond of Lottie even though we never met her—it isn't easy for a ninety-year-old woman to maintain a farm, so we are completely sympathetic to the circumstances that led to the farm's condition. But you haven't lived until you've extracted a litter of possums from under your floor.

We stayed in an apartment in Boerne while we worked over the farm. Out came more than a mile of rusty barbed-wire fence, and in went more than a mile of new 9-39 fencing on cedar posts. We tore Lottie's farmhouse back to its frame and started over, installing new electrical, plumbing, heat, air conditioning, walls—the works. Weeks were spent scraping ball moss out of the live oaks and post oaks, and trimming up their gothic, neglected limbs. A bounty of invasive Mexican Hat was mowed and mowed again. And again. We applied dozens and dozens—probably hundreds—of pounds of fire ant poison. A new 460-foot-deep well. New septic system.

We fertilized the worn pastures back into normalcy and seeded them with native grasses. The fellows who drilled the new well climbed the windmill derrick and lubricated its 1940 Chicago Aermotor gears. We used our brand-new John Deere tractor to tear out the chain-link fence that Lottie had put around her garden to exclude the deer. (We figured that no self-respecting deer would be deterred by a chain-link fence, anyway.) One day we had five men in Kevlar moon suits come out and yank all the pink asbestos siding off the farmhouse. We replaced it with cedar, which we allowed to turn gray in the weather.

We figured out that a big concrete slab near the house—the size of a very, very firm queen-sized mattress—was capping a disused well, even older than the one under the windmill. After moving aside some rocks that covered a hole in the center of the slab, I found that the well was hand-dug: I could see the stones lining its five-foot diameter. Jeanne bought me an old-fashioned hand-pump for my birthday, and we had the well-and-windmill guys plumb and attach it. The well turned out to be only about sixty-five feet deep, and it has water only in the spring, but that's not the point.

We stocked the farm with nine goats, and by the following spring they had turned themselves into eighteen. This was the rural, simple life. That is, if you disregard the fact that we had nine internal combustion engines: two SUVs, a pickup truck, a beat-up roadster, a tractor, riding mower, push mower, weed whip and chainsaw. We also acquired a disk harrow, seed broadcaster, boom sprayer, straight blade, grass shredder and more electric power tools than you can find in your typical Home Depot.

Seven-foot-high piles of brush, prickly pears and scrap lumber made bonfires on a cold, wet morning. We left two more brush piles the size of small houses in place for the birds and critters to enjoy. There was a lot of hard work involved. We soon learned to buy the biggest, baddest version of any gear we needed: the economy version wouldn't last a week on our place.

While cleaning out the barns we came across lots of stuff worth keeping. A broken blue Mason jar, two-thirds of a cream separator, a burlap sack full of rusty coffee cans... treasures like that. A tattered box held sheaves of greeting cards, letters and postcards that Lottie had received. We put all this aside, dedicating one room of the old log barn to what we called the "Lottie Kohls Memorial Art Gallery and Museum."

Back when we lived in cities, we bought and sold more than our share of houses, new and old. The experience is not at all like buying a farm. Or at least it's not at all like buying a farm that has been allowed to decline into semi-charming disrepair. Unlike your basic high-rise condominium, Lottie's place hadn't been swept clean of all evidence of the prior owners. If anything, it positively boasted of its heritage. But it boasted in an ambiguous, obscure way that left us certain that the heritage was there without giving more than a few clues about what it might be.

The most intriguing building on the property was the old log barn. The Kohls' real estate agent told us that it dated back to the mid-1850s, but we had a sense that he was winging it.

On close inspection, the barn—which the Kohls had used for storing hay—appeared to have done service as a cabin at one time. It was built in dogtrot style—two square log modules with a roofed breezeway between—but there was a stone addition on the back that closed off the dogtrot. In the front of the cabin were animal pens, almost certainly an original feature, since the early German settlers combined home and barn in the European style.

We could see that the corrugated metal roof had been installed over old cedar shingles. The shingles were nailed into rough-sawn cypress planks. There were still distinct chisel marks on the stone part of the cabin: irregular, uneven marks that distinguished handwork, not power chisels.

The wind blew between gaps in the logwork where the chinking had fallen out. We learned later that this large-gap style was part of the German architectural vernacular: they spaced their logs widely, and used chunks of stone bound with kiln-burned lime mortar to fill the interstices.

A large, square hole in the wall and a rectangle cut in the cypress plank floor evidenced a long-gone hearth. Logs sagged into the hole where the fireplace had been.

Some of the windows boasted well-crafted but long-neglected casement windows. They looked odd set into hand-hewn cedar logs. We learned later that this, too was characteristic of German Hill Country pioneer homes; one of the first local industries to emerge was the manufacture of cased doors and windows, for which the tidy Germans had a preference. There were door and window makers in New Braunfels among the first waves of colonists.

It was the old log barn, or more properly the old log-and-stone cabin, that caught my imagination. We knew that the Kohls had bought the farm more than sixty years ago from the Toepperweins, who were said to have lived on the land for generations. The cabin obviously dated back to the Toepperwein era. A few months after buying the place, we learned that the Toepperwein family included a couple of famous trick-shot artists that toured with Wild West Shows. Lottie Kohls began to fade; we started telling friends that we lived on the old Toepperwein homestead. We dubbed the farm historic, and I began digging around to figure out just who had built this farm outside Boerne, and what kind of world they lived in.

Let me tell you what I learned.

Maps

The Texas Hill Country

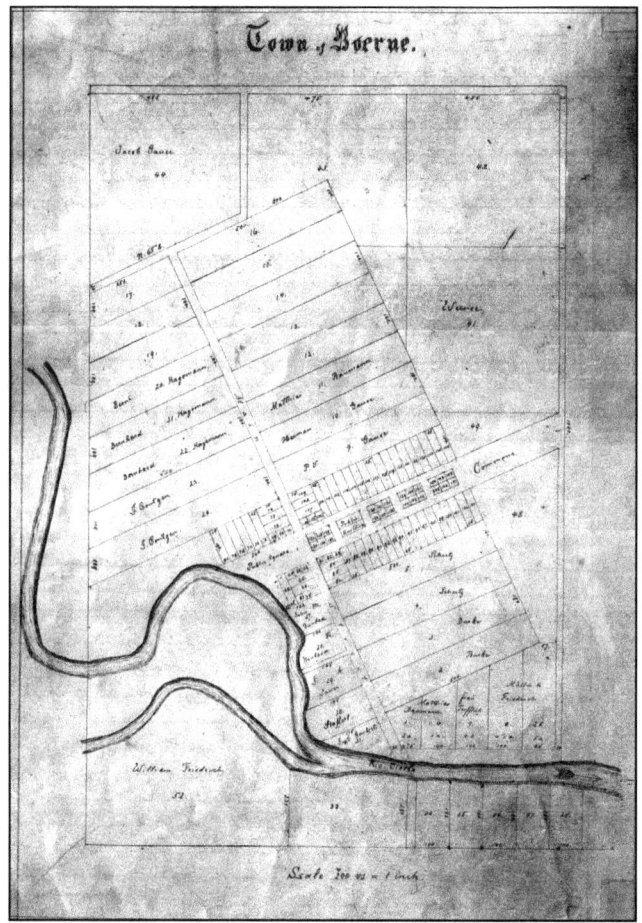

The original Boerne townsite plat. Names of lot owners (or potential purchasers) inscribed on the plat include Jacob Sauer, Bernhard Hagemann, J. Contgen, Matthias Baumann, Schertz, Herman Saner, P. V. Saner, John M. Dundan, Fr. Neubauer, Staffel, Gust. Sombert, William Friedrich, Trefflich and Mueller.

A more legible version of the original townsite plat, with a few of today's streets labeled for orientation. Notice the paucity of streets in town; the only lateral off Main Street is Newton Alley, meant to provide access to Cibolo Creek for animal watering and bucket brigades.

Hill Country

The rolling hills that surround Boerne are covered with oak and cedar, enclosing flat, green bottoms coursed by prolific spring-fed creeks and rivers. Deer, wild turkey and fox inhabit the forests and venture into the fields at dusk. Four distinct but moderate seasons reinforce the cycles of life.

Geographically, the Texas Hill Country is the rippling eastern portion of the Edwards Plateau. It is bordered to the west by less convoluted stretches of the plateau, to the south by the Balcones Escarpment, and to the north by rolling plains and prairies that extend to the base of the Llano Estacado. The Colorado River is a reasonable definition of the eastern boundary, though the hills don't extend that far in places. The Hill Country is not especially high: its maximum elevation is around thirteen hundred feet above the sea and much of it lies below one thousand feet.

Like the remainder of the Edwards Plateau, the Hill Country has a thin layer of soil over Comanchean limestone. This same limestone underpins the High Plains of Texas; despite the ripples in the Hill Country, the plateau is considered the southernmost unit of the Great Plains. Cotton and other crops have been raised in the Hill Country, but the scant local soil lends itself more to grazing. Cattle do well where soils are deepest and forage is greatest. Sheep are the livestock of choice as soils and flora thin; goats are the best alternative as hillsides become rockier and grasses turn into browse.

It may be limestone that most characterizes the Hill Country. Subsurface aquifers flow through limestone, making the waters exceptionally hard. Houses are built of limestone blocks. Long limestone fences divide fields. They've been quarrying limestone out of the face of the Balcones Escarpment for more than a century and, while the resulting scars are far from attractive, they've barely made a dent in the supply of stone. As you travel northward in the Hill Country, the foundation changes from limestone to granite, signaling that you are nearing its northern limits.

Limestone makes the spring-fed creeks and rivers of the Hill Country run clear and cool. The waters are overhung with live oaks and post oaks. The most beautiful streams—the Guadalupe River and Cibolo Creek, for example—are lined with towering cypress trees that thrust immense roots into the cool current.

The first human inhabitants of the Hill Country were a people that we call Paleoindians, who probably arrived about twelve thousand years ago. These natives survived by hunting large herd animals—mammoths and giant bison. Their principal hunting tools were clumsy thrusting spears, which limited their ability to capture smaller game. They supplemented their diets by gathering local plants, seeds, nuts and berries. Paleoindians followed the animal herds, living under rock ledges, in caves and in crude man-made shelters.

Around eight thousand years ago the Paleoindian culture made a gradual segue into the Archaic Indian Period. From that time until about A.D. 1200 Texas natives adapted to the disappearance of large land mammals by diversifying their diets, learning to hunt and trap smaller game and expanding their tool inventory. Archaic natives were true hunter-gatherers, remaining in one place for long periods and seasonally cycling through known hunting grounds. They used the spear-throwing stick called an atlatl, were adept at snaring small game, learned to catch fish with hooks and nets and used flat, curved throwing sticks to take rabbits. Women gathered grapes, berries, turnips, wild onions, plums, nuts and prickly pear tunas.

Over the centuries, natives learned to grow crops. Squash became a dietary staple, and gourds were the makings of spoons, dippers and water vessels. Sunflowers, little barley, sumpweed and other simple crops supplemented the foods that the natives obtained by hunting and gathering. Around A.D. 700 corn and beans arrived with nomads from the south, but did not make a significant dietary impact for several hundred more years. Eventually Hill Country natives—like natives throughout North America—became dependent upon the three sisters—corns, beans and squash—for much of their nutrition.

Population densities were extremely light during the Paleoindian and Archaic Periods. In early centuries there may have been only a few hundred people in all of Texas, growing to a few thousand, then a few tens of thousands. Increases in population reflected improvements in diet; as people learned to farm, and as their hunting efficiency increased, more survived and larger communities became sustainable.

Toward the end of the Archaic Period, Texas natives began developing languages, belief systems and traditions. They formed themselves into clans and developed a sense of cultural identity. By perhaps A.D. 1500 early Texans had assumed the clan and tribal identities that early Spanish and French explorers encountered.

So far as we know, five hundred years ago the Texas Hill Country was a sort of no-man's land—a buffer zone and hunting ground for surrounding groups. Identifiable native communities lived to the south, east and west, and other native clans were moving down from the north, but the Hill Country was largely unclaimed. This is not to say that it was unoccupied, for archaeological evidence confirms that there was at least some minimal native population, and nomads and hunters must have passed through, but it is fair to say that no one group of natives had truly settled in the region.

Over the next century or two, Coahuiltecans from Mexico and Karankawas from the Gulf Coast began moving north. Jumanos, originally denizens of New Mexico and far West Texas, extended their nomadic boundaries to the east across almost the entire state. Groups living between the Brazos and San Antonio Rivers gradually coalesced into a clan of people known as the Tonkawas and spread northward. Still, though, the Hill Country remained marginally settled territory.

That began to change as Athapaskan natives moved southward out of Canada across the western Great Plains. A group that came to be known as the Lipan Apaches moved south and eventually settled in the Southern Plains of Texas. As Lipans migrated south, they traversed the Hill Country, which became one of their hunting grounds. Soon Apaches came under pressure from Comanches, who were in turn under pressure from Cheyennes and other plains tribes. The most common Comanche bands in Central Texas were the Penetakas.

Apaches and Comanches were horseback hunters and raiders. They aggressively claimed the plains buffalo trade as their own and defended their territory against European intrusions. These two groups of natives ranged far and wide; though Lipan Apaches and Penetaka Comanches are often thought of as denizens of Central Texas, in autumn and winter they (and other Comanches and Apaches) raided much farther south, deep into Mexico.

The North America that Europeans encountered was not a trackless frontier. Native migration and hunting, and an extended commercial network for trading pots, baskets, points, turquoise, copper and other goods, left established trails that Europeans followed in their explorations. In the first half of the sixteenth century Alvar Nuñez Cabeza de Vaca traveled with natives along trails extending the breadth of Texas and beyond. The routes that Spaniards adopted in moving north across the Rio Grande into Texas followed traditional native pathways.

Two important native trails were in the vicinity of Boerne, known to the Spanish as the Pinta Trail and the Camino Viejo. Both were networks of pathways, not definitive single traces. I am among those who have repeated the traditional lore that Boerne was established at the point where the Pinta

Trail crossed Cibolo Creek. The latest research establishes otherwise.

The Pinta Trail, which connected the region that is now San Antonio to today's Sisterdale and Fredericksburg, was eight miles to the east of Boerne, crossing Cibolo Creek at its junction with Post Oak Creek, then taking a rugged track over hill and dale northwest to cross the Guadalupe River near Sisterdale. The trail was part of the return path taken on a 1767 frontier inspection by the Marques de Rubí. Early German immigrants used the Pinta Trail for travel from New Braunfels to Fredericksburg, but it did not become an established wagon road. The trail has been abandoned and forgotten except for some roadways within Camp Stanley, identifiable traces to the north, below Cibolo Creek, and a few miles of FM 1376 from the Guadalupe River to the headwaters of West Sister Creek. Its entire path is discernable only from original Texas land surveys that note its location.

The Camino Viejo ran from where San Antonio is today 180 miles northwest and beyond, into the far frontier. The Spanish followed the Camino Viejo into the wilderness and established the Santa Cruz de San Saba Mission and the San Luis de las Amarillas Presidio near today's Menard, and the trail was sometimes referred to as the San Saba Road. When Jack Hays and Samuel Highsmith unsuccessfully tried to open a road from San Antonio to El Paso in 1848, the Camino Viejo was the first leg of their journey; as military forts were built along its path and settlers used it to migrate west, it became known as the Immigrant Road or the Upper Military Road.

The Camino Viejo began in the vicinity of central San Antonio, long before there was a central San Antonio. It was a place where a network of native trails from the south and east converged. From there, the trail tracked northwest toward where Interstate Highway 10 now enters a gap in the Balcones Escarpment, below Exit 555. From there to Boerne, it generally followed the line of the Interstate, passing just west of the original Boerne townsite before taking a now-closed route over Spanish Pass (also known as "Porto Viejo"), then angling to the northwest to cross the Guadalupe River just west of the mouth of Block Creek, in the vicinity of the still-standing but abandoned San Antonio & Aransas Pass Railway bridge, before following Block Creek to the route that became Old No. 9 and proceeding to Fredericksburg via Cain City. The trail was better known to early settlers as the Fredericksburg Road, a name that later was applied to Old No. 9.

Just as there is local lore that mis-locates the Pinta Trail, so is there lore that routes the Camino Viejo beyond Boerne to the west of its actual route, running by Comfort and Kerrville on the way to Menard. That is a geographically tempting route, and there were important native and Spanish trails to the west, but no evidence has surfaced to indicate that the Camino Viejo took that route.

The original Boerne townsite is a few hundred yards east of the old Camino Viejo in an elbow of Cibolo Creek near the confluence of Frederick Creek (originally Friedrich's Creek). The now-vanished Camino Viejo would be inside today's city limits; it crossed Johns Road near the driveway to H. W. Schwope and Sons Water Well Drilling. Once Boerne was established, a new path diverted through the settlement and eventually became the main route north from San Antonio.

Not long after Boerne was platted in 1852, settlers carved a wagon road to Sisterdale along today's FM 1376, creating a cutoff to the Pinta Trail crossing of the Guadalupe River; the lower Pinta Trail was falling into disuse by that time, probably because its rugged route was difficult for wagons, and the upper Pinta Trail was soon replaced by a gentler route to the east that FM 1376 follows today. Though the road did extend all the way to Fredericksburg, it was known as the Sisterdale Road.

When settlers first arrived in Boerne, both of its creeks were abundant spring-fed resources—their banks were an excellent choice for a townsite. Today, upstream diversion and use, combined with ongoing aquifer depletion, have reduced both to rainwater drainages that are sometimes little more than a trickle.

In Boerne, Cibolo Creek looks more like a river, or a lake, because it was dammed for William Dietert's mill; the mill pond is attractive and has long outlasted the mill, having been restored by the city decades after the mill ceased operations.

The Coahuiltecans called Cibolo Creek Xoloton; the Tonkawas knew it as Bata Coniquiyoqui. In 1691 Father Damian Massanet dubbed it Santa Crecencia while on his way to found the first Franciscan missions in East Texas. On the same trip, Domingo Teran de los Rios named it San Ignacio de Loyola. By 1716 Domingo Ramon called it San Xavier.

The word "cibolo" means buffalo in Spanish, but there is more to the story. When Cabeza de Vaca finally reached Mexico City after his seven-year trek across Texas and Mexico, he told stories of a gold-laden, jewel-encrusted empire to the north: the Seven Cities of Cibola. In 1540, Francisco Vasquez de Coronado set forth into the wilderness searching for the legendary civilization. The Seven Cities of Cibola turned out to be a few dusty Zuni villages in New Mexico, and they had no gold. The search for the elusive Cibola turned into a joke. Spaniards began to call the prolific buffalo that they found on their journey—previously known as *vacas*, or cows—cibolas. A cibola is a buffalo cow, cibolo a bull.

Germans

The first Germans in the Texas Hill Country were economic refugees spawned by two decades of German political and social unrest that began during the 1830s. From 1844 through 1846 a quasi-charitable society of German nobles known as the Adelsverein (Noble's Association), reacting to circumstances in Europe, tried to export proletariat and peasantry to a better life in Texas while implanting an improved political state (and a potential trading partner) in a new land; for at least some Adelsverein members, a sub rosa ambition was to carve a German colony out of the Republic of Texas.

The Adelsverein brought thousands of immigrants ashore on the west end of Matagorda Bay, at a site they called Carlshaven. That landing later became the town of Indianola, which was destroyed twice by hurricanes and ultimately abandoned.

From Carlshaven, the German immigrants proceeded across the prairies of South Texas by wagon and on foot. Their initial destination was a spot on the Comal River that their leader, Prince Carl of Solms-Braunfels, purchased as a way station and named after his home town.

The first group of colonists under the guidance of Prince Solms amounted to a few hundred souls. They made their 1845 trip with a great deal of difficulty—many made the journey on foot because wagons were scarce—but no disasters. The next year the Adelsverein put management of the colony in the hands of John O. Meusebach and sent over more than five thousand new colonists. The number was far beyond the verein's capacity to finance, manage or transport, and the situation worsened when war broke out between the United States and Mexico, resulting in every serviceable wagon being called into military duty. The spring of 1846 was unusually cold and wet, and the colonists were stranded at Carlshaven, unable to cross the boggy prairies. Transportation shortages resulted in many of them staying on the coast into the summer season of mosquitoes and fevers.

Young Bernard Monken, who eventually established a ranch south of Boerne and is buried in the Boerne Cemetery, was one of those who made the trek in 1846. He arrived in Carlshaven with his parents, a brother and two sisters. Though promised housing and transportation by the Adelsverein, after their fifty-eight-day voyage across the Atlantic they were first stranded on Matagorda Island in December when their ship ran aground, then left on the coast, living in a mud-and-grass hut until July. The conditions were miserable.

When an opportunity arose, the Monkens sent daughter Rose ahead to New Braunfels with friends, hoping she could find employment there. Finally, tired of waiting at Carlshaven, paterfamilias Friedrich Monken decided to walk to New Braunfels to seek accommodations and transport. While Friedrich was gone, the remaining Monkens were told that they would be going on the next wagon to depart. Sixteen people from three related families—the Monkens, the Fietsams and the Webers—and their belongings left Carlshaven on July 5 on a single wagon.

They made it to the colony's first trail camp in one day, but the next day their overloaded wagon broke a wheel in the middle of an open prairie. They procured a substitute wagon and a yoke of oxen from a nearby landowner, hoping to ride to the next watering place, where they could make arrangements for the repair of their broken wagon.

While at the watering hole on the verein's trail, father Friedrich Monken crossed their path on his return from New Braunfels with a wagon. Now they had three wagons, one broken, one borrowed. The elder Monken sent his good wagon to Carlshaven, and went with his family in the borrowed wagon to repair the broken wheel on their original wagon, leading Bernard Monken to conclude that his father had "made his trip on foot to New Braunfels all in vain."

After another breakdown and repair, the Monkens pulled into Victoria—a trip of forty miles in fourteen days. All of the group were sickly and covered in mosquito bites from their journey.

The Monkens made it to the town of Spring Creek, where their teamster inexplicably departed with the wagon and team. Meat and vegetables were not available; the family lived on corn meal left in their barrel. Soon Bernard Monken's mother died of a disease contracted on the coast. Monken, led by his grieving father and accompanied by his sickly brother Henry and his sister Barbara, carried on.

Another teamster took pity on the families and transported them as far as where Hochheim is today. Again they were stranded. Henry Monken soon took sick.

The Monkens turned in desperation to a nearby merchant named Burkhart, offering to pay liberally for transport to New Braunfels. A local youth volunteered to serve as teamster and obtained two yoke of oxen, adding them to two of his own, and began the trek north. Burkhart kindly accompanied them on the first leg of the journey. The wagon bogged down crossing Peach Creek; Burkhart and the young drover went back to get more teams. It began to rain. The creek rose, threatening the Monkens' belongings. Providentially, two wagons appeared from the north. On one wagon—as if written in a Hollywood script—was Rose. Hearing stories in New Braunfels of the misery sweeping Carlshaven, she had hired a teamster and, along with another wagon heading south, had gone to find her family.

The southbound teamsters extricated the Monkens' wagon from Peach Creek, but not before also extricating a portion of the family's dwindling funds. One wagon continued south, while the family made arrangements with the teamster brought by Rose.

That teamster took the family two miles to a cotton gin owned by a family named Jones. Then, under the pretense of looking for more oxen, the teamster vanished, stranding the family yet again. They wrote to Burkhart for help, giving the note to a passing traveler. While they waited, young Henry Monken died of a fever brought from the coast, and a child of the Jones family took sick. Rose volunteered to ride to Gonzales for a doctor. On her way back, her horse reared and fell on her, the saddle pommel striking her in the chest. Seriously injured, she barely made it back to her family.

Burkhart sent a man with two yoke of oxen to take the Monkens to New Braunfels. Rose, the wounded angel of mercy, died during a brief layover in Seguin. It was September by the time the remaining Monkens—father Friedrich, son Bernard and daughter Barbara—reached New Braunfels. Shortly after arriving, Fate put the finishing touch on their brutal journey: Barbara died of fever and was buried there.

Six Monkens had departed Carlshaven in July, after fifty-eight days at sea and more than six months of misery on the coast. It had taken them ninety days to travel to New Braunfels, in a tortuous journey that saw them repeatedly stranded by unscrupulous teamsters and beset by disease and death. Only two—Bernard Monken and his father Friedrich—survived.

After the arduous trek from Carlshaven, most Adelsverein colonists began building temporary homes in New Braunfels. Some decided to go no further, and built more permanent dwellings. But many pushed north to Fredericksburg. They meant to colonize a vast land grant made by the Republic of Texas, known as the Fisher-Miller Grant. Under the terms of that grant, the Adelsverein could earn land for its colonists (and for itself) by settling at least two thousand families within the grant.

But the Fisher-Miller Grant was north of the Llano River, deep into Comanche Territory. Although the second leader of the Adelsverein, John O. Meusebach, reached a historic peace treaty with the Comanches, the land grant ultimately proved too far into the wilderness to be settled within the deadlines established by Texas. Fredericksburg was the farthest successful settlement of the Adelsverein, unless you count the tiny hamlet of Castell, which today sits just south of the Llano and was abandoned more than once after Comanche depredations.

As the Adelsverein cast about for ways to accomplish its goals, it enlisted a group of young men from Darmstadt, Germany, who became known as "the Forty," though their numbers were a bit less than thirty-five. They were few, but their impact was significant and they brought with them an intense political and social philosophy. More than the Adelsverein's organizers, they valued individual freedom and had an idealistic view of the potential for a new society in a new land, viewing the world through the communal lenses of Saint-Simon, Fourier and Cabet. In contrast to how twentieth century communism evolved, however, these idealists saw society as capable of self-governance without central authority. Their communism was a benign, rational, free-will society of people contributing according to their abilities and interests. These were top-down utopian socialists of the French stripe, not bottom-up, revolutionary, class-struggle communists of the Karl Marx school.

The Forty crossed the Llano and established a communal camp known as Bettina. As was the case with the original Castell townsite, it was just a few hundred feet into the Fisher-Miller Grant. Three other towns—Meerholz, Leiningen and Schoenburg—were likewise established just over the grant's border, but disappeared quickly under Comanche pressure and frontier hardships. Bettina never had a chance to survive—its communal idealism proved entirely unsuited to frontier Texas, where self-reliance, initiative, individualism and hard work were the keys to survival.

In the Hill Country, the economic, political and social experiments of the colonists and the communalists did not turn out well. The Adelsverein's naively conceived colony collapsed under the financial realities of frontier settlement. The Forty's commune at Bettina foundered on the most basic elements of human nature (nobody wanted to do the work; everyone wanted to manage). But these failures were not the end of German settlement in the Texas Hill Country. In a way, they were only the beginning, for once Germans were liberated from the expectation of free land within the Fisher-

Miller Grant, once they were disabused of the notion that the Adelsverein would support them in some way, once they had only themselves to rely on (and once many of them realized that they were stuck in Texas without the means to return to Germany), their horizons expanded and they sought new ways to become successful settlers.

The Adelsverein colonists and the Forty were followed by refugees from an abortive 1848 revolution in Germany. Known as the Forty-Eighters, these immigrants fueled a new surge of expansion into the Hill Country. The colonists brought by the Adelsverein had been primarily working-class Germans, though there were a number of leaders and adventurers of the noble class among them. The Forty were all educated young men of a liberal political bent. Most Forty-Eighters fled Germany because they had supported liberal democratic changes to governance by enlightened despots—and because their attempt to change the system had failed, making them persona non grata. As advocates of democracy, the Forty-Eighters were not necessarily in favor of extending the vote to the uneducated classes, but they felt that a parliamentary system—dominated by nobles, academics and the educated—should replace despotism. Thus, where the Adelsverein colonists were primarily economic refugees and the Forty were primarily communal idealists, the Forty-Eighters were for the most part liberal political refugees who favored an elitist democratic form of government.

The Germans who arrived early in Boerne were a mix of all three groups—Adelsverein colonists, the Forty and Forty-Eighters—but it was the Forty and the Forty-Eighters who most influenced its development.

Founding

Czech descendant Ludovic Colquhoun was born in Virginia; in 1837 he moved to San Antonio, where he became a successful lawyer and land speculator. He was a senator of the Republic of Texas, a member of the anti-Houston contingent and a part of the faction that favored war with Mexico. Colquhoun became entangled with the legendary Samuel Maverick in a dispute over a piece of property on Cibolo Creek. In 1842, while they were in court battling it out, Mexican General Adrian Woll raided San Antonio, taking everyone at the courthouse hostage. Colquhoun and Maverick were imprisoned in infamous Perote Prison and released in 1844 upon the intervention of the U. S. Ambassador to Mexico.

Colquhoun returned to his San Antonio land business. By 1845—when a second wave of Adelsverein colonists was coming ashore at Carlshaven—he and his partner William H. Steele had gathered headright certificates for more than 170,000 acres of land. In that year the partnership dissolved, with the lion's share of the assets going to Colquhoun, and he used one of his certificates—purchased from Maria Ynacia Leal in 1837—to claim two-thirds of a league and two-thirds of a labor of land (more than three thousand acres) on Cibolo Creek, about thirty miles northwest of San Antonio. The land was assigned survey number 180 in Bexar section three.

Colquhoun was savvy. The land was wooded, gently rolling acreage along a particularly beautiful stretch of Cibolo Creek. The Camino Viejo approached from the south and ran just to the west of his tract, almost touching the southwest corner. There was a flat stretch through the center of Colquhoun's land that would make excellent farms.

But it was 1845. There were few settlers in the Hill Country except at New Braunfels. Colquhoun's purchase was pure speculation. His fellow land speculator and Bexar surveyor John James acquired the tract from Colquhoun almost immediately after Colquhoun secured a patent from the Republic of Texas. In all likelihood, this transaction was part of a larger arrangement in which James provided surveying services on a great many Colquhoun tracts (for a survey was necessary before a patent could issue) in exchange for a portion of the land surveyed. Given James's extensive travels in the Hill Country as a surveyor, it may be that he—more than Colquhoun—appreciated the strategic location of Survey 180, as evidenced by James's assembly of several more parcels of land in the vicinity.

In May 1850 James sold four hundred acres of land immediately west of Survey 180, straddling the Camino Viejo, to Wilhelm Friedrich for four hundred dollars. Two months later James sold 1,330 acres in the southwest corner of Survey 180, adjacent to Friedrich's land, to Christian Hesse. Hesse's land sat where the town of Boerne is today.

Friedrich and Hesse had both been part of the Forty's Bettina experiment. Soon four other members of the Forty (Christian Flach, Adam Vogt, Leopold Schulz and Phillip Zoeller) joined Friedrich in building a small compound on his property. Their habitations sat on a knoll about a half-mile from Cibolo Creek, adjacent to the Camino Viejo. Darmstadt medical student Friedrich Kramer arrived soon. Almost unbelievably, they were attempting to found another commune.

The group on Friedrich's farm called their humble camp "Tusculum," the same as Cicero's country home. We know few specifics about the Texas version of Tusculum except its location, west of Cibolo Creek and north of Johns Road. Subsequent owners built new buildings and tore down old ones. A doctor named Crosky, who was also a surveyor and land trader, used a building there during the early twentieth century. A ten-foot-deep excavation by owner Hugh Schwope uncovered stone curbing that once rimmed a Tusculum spring.

Friedrich's ownership of Tusculum lasted eight months; Adam Vogt bought the land from him in January 1851 for sixteen hundred dollars. The fourfold increase in price from Friedrich to Vogt probably reflected the value of improvements made under Friedrich's ownership, and may have included some livestock.

Vogt may have accommodated the idealistic gathering of Darmstadters for a time after he bought the land, but no one claims that Tusculum survived for more than a year or two as a commune. There is some uncertainty about exactly who was present at Tusculum: Even though he was nearby, Hesse is not considered a member, because he had his own farm; Boerne businessman Rudolph Carstanjen and Fredericksburg fixture Jacob Kuechler are said by some to have been present, but supporting facts are scant.

Across the Cibolo from Tusculum, Christian Hesse planned to farm—or possibly develop—his 1,330 acres with his brother. His aim was frustrated when his sibling did not come to Texas. Around the time that Tusculum faded, Hesse decided to leave Texas (for Australia, the county records say, but this may be a mis-transcription of "Austria"). Some loose ends had to be cleared up first. He struck a deal in May 1852 re-combining his choice tract with John James's land so that they each owned an undivided one-half interest in all of Survey 180. Then he reached an agreement with Gustav Theissen of San Antonio under which Hesse gave his half interest plus $1,140 to Theissen in return for Theissen agreeing to pay off several promissory notes that Hesse had outstanding. Because Hesse was leaving North America, he gave a power of attorney to his fellow member of the Forty, Ferdinand Herff, authorizing him to deliver a deed to Theissen once the loans were paid.

When Theissen bought into Survey 180 in May 1852 he and John James already had an agreement, reached the month before, to divide and sell the land. In July James filed a survey plat laying out Boerne's town lots and outlots (oversized tracts on the periphery of town meant for a farm, not a residence). Circumstances had changed since Ludovic Colquhoun first patented the land. The U. S. Army had built Fort Martin Scott outside of Fredericksburg, securing the Camino Viejo—by then better known locally as the Fredericksburg Road—from San Antonio north and opening what would become the Upper Military Road to Fort McKavett, Fort Lancaster, distant Fort Fillmore and El Paso. Soon a stage line commenced service between San Antonio and El Paso, following the old Camino Viejo before turning west. Boerne was a day's ride north from San Antonio—a stream-crossing where stables, inns, stores and taverns were sure to sprout.

James and Theissen took the initiative to develop Boerne, but it would be a mistake to think of them as the only people who understood the area's potential. Adam Vogt had already settled into some of James's other land. After selling his interest in Tusculum to Vogt, Wilhelm Friedrich stayed in the vicinity and bought more land, including a forty-four-acre outlot in the southwest corner of the Boerne survey. Boerne's Friedrich Creek ran across Friedrich's farm, thus its name. (During the Civil War Friedrich was employed by the Confederacy to build and operate a gunpowder plant in San Antonio; he died when it exploded.)

John N. Simon Menger, who had just opened a soap and candle factory in San Antonio—its first manufacturing plant—invested in 1280 acres across Cibolo Creek to the south of town, and sold that tract to Joseph Bergmann in 1853. Bergmann sold off some of the acreage along what became South Main Street and farmed the remainder for many years; he and his wife Teresa raised six children there.

Physician Ferdinand Herff, a prominent member of the Forty, was already investing in the area, purchasing a choice 320 acres on the Cibolo in 1852 and 640 acres just south of the Tusculum site in 1854 (he would split that acreage with Wilhelm Friedrich in 1856). Herff remained a resident of San Antonio, but the Boerne area became his private retreat and a place where he invested heavily, purchasing ten thousand Hill Country acres over time and involving himself in numerous Boerne civic causes.

Boerne was not an instant success, taking more than a decade to show staying power. Early purchasers of town lots from James and Theissen included Johann Burke (1852) and Mathias Baumann (1853). Burke sold his two Boerne lots to Julius Fabra four months after buying them. Fabra farmed and freighted locally, and in 1857 he began butchering livestock.

Fabra did not wait for customers to come to him for meat. He would slaughter cattle in the afternoon, butcher them early the next morning, load the beef on a two-wheel horse-drawn cart and make the trip through town, shouting "meat!" Boerne's milkman would follow a similar route with a high cart holding ten-gallon cans of milk. According to Max Theis, "You could go out with your pitcher and he would fill it for a dime, whether it was a half gallon or a gallon. It didn't make any difference."

Thirty years later Julius Fabra opened a butcher shop and smokehouse that evolved into a grocery and meat market, then passed into the hands of his son Ludwig and his grandson Henry. The Fabra market became such a Boerne institution that the two-story smokehouse was preserved and granted a Texas historical marker. It still stands behind a wing of the large limestone building at Main Street and Rosewood Avenue that was once the Boerne State Bank and is now dubbed "Boerne Center."

Mathias Baumann opened a blacksmith shop near where Boerne's Main Street crossed the Cibolo. It was the first business in town. It wasn't long before Baumann had competition. Philip Jacob Theis arrived in 1858 and began work as a blacksmith and wheelwright. To house his wife Margaretha and seven children, Theis built a house in the Tejano "palisado" style—willow reeds woven among cedar uprights, then plastered with adobe mud and topped with a thatched roof. This unusual structure still stands on Newton Street, just west of Main Street. (Newton Street is just a stub, meant to provide a public alley to Cibolo Creek that the bucket brigade could use to fight fires.) Philip Theis conducted his blacksmithing under a mulberry tree in the front yard, where a building now stands. His son August took over the family business, continued living in the house with his wife Agnes and—like his father before him—raised seven children.

Early purchasers of Boerne outlots were Patterson D. Saner and August Trefflich, who took title to their land in 1854. Saner spent his first few Hill Country years at a shingle-making camp in Bandera. After arriving in Boerne, he farmed, freighted and involved himself in community affairs, serving over the years as constable, judge, justice of the peace and postmaster.

Trefflich bought his lot for sixty dollars, sold it in 1855 to Andreas Blum for $175, and Blum sold it to William Vogt (no relation to Adam Vogt) in 1856 for two hundred dollars. Vogt and his wife Ernestine had come ashore at Indianola in 1852, and lived in Seguin until buying their Boerne tract from Blum. In 1859 they purchased forty more acres on the edge of Boerne, where they built a one-room log cabin. Then they built another one-room cabin, and a third. The three sat side-by-side, each with its own entrance but under a common roof, making it an unusual double-dogtrot design that still stands on Plant Street.

William Dietert was an important early arrival in Boerne. Hugo Clauss, who was in Boerne almost from the beginning, tells us what change Dietert wrought: "We had to pulverize corn with a hand axe. One could not mill the corn in our coffee grinders because the corn was too hard for that. Then an American joined the settlement and brought with him a metal corngrinder. Now we had corn meal, though it wouldn't be called that today.

"Soon a miller [William Dietert] arrived and built the first flour mill and sawmill on the Cibolo. You could exchange your corn for fine corn flour. What progress for the young settlement, since we now had decent cornbread." Building Dietert's mill involved constructing a dam across the Cibolo for water power, backing the creek up into an attractive mill pond in the center of town.

Clauss also tells us about the (possibly greater) importance of August Staffel, who arrived around 1853. Staffel began Boerne's first store, but it wasn't much. According to Clauss, Staffel had worked as a survey chain man for John

James, and as payment for his services took a few town lots, "upon which he built a hut covered with long reeds." Soon Staffel was running a store from his shanty. Clauss says, "Naturally Sundays everybody gathered at August Staffel's, where people hatched plans for the future and told hunting and Indian stories."

"During our meetings we had only Schnapps. The German national drink—beer—was missed very much, as you can imagine. Friend Staffel brewed something out of corn and sugar, etc., which he called beer. For lack of anything better we drank that and smoked a cigar imported by a Mr. Rexroth from Bremen, who had given it to August because it was extremely cheap, or perhaps August had to take it to satisfy a debt."

The beer drought did not last forever. In 1855 William Menger opened the Western Brewery on Alamo Square in San Antonio. Clauss reported that "although most of us had some doubt that beer could be brewed in Texas, it was welcome news that the brewery was operational and the beer on the market. Friend Staffel brought the first little keg from San Antonio, for testing, he said.

"On Sunday the keg was ceremoniously put on the table, adorned with oak leaves and flowers and tapped. We stood around the small barrel and held a glass of beer after years of deprivation; we sang German songs and danced around the barrel until the litmus test was emptied.

"With this first barrel, we also laid the foundation for the Boerne Gesangverein [singing club], which still exists today."

Clauss was writing in 1882; the gesangverein—formally organized by Karl Dienger in 1860—endured until 1976. There is an 1860 picture of its twelve members in formal attire. They include such familiar names as Anton Bergmann (son of farmer Joseph Bergmann), William Vogt, William Dietert and his brother Henry Dietert. Also present is Herman Toepperwein, son of Lucian Toepperwein, who originally settled along Grape Creek; several of the Toepperweins moved to Boerne. Oddly absent is August Staffel, but there is stout, solid Hugo Clauss with a bushy beard and a receding hairline.

The keg of beer that August Staffel imported from San Antonio grew into a Boerne institution—Staffel's Tavern. Clauss said that in early years "every stranger under the straw roof of the Mexican jacal was greeted and strengthened, since in this little store one could get a drink of firewater, the only one between San Antonio and Fredericksburg." Later, when the tavern had added solid walls and a floor, people said that they could set their clocks to noon when Adam Vogt headed to Staffel's tavern to spend the afternoon reading and talking with friends.

The Boerne Gesangverein became more than a singing club; it became a gene pool. Anton Bergmann had four sisters. Rosa married William Dietert. Amalie married Henry Dietert. Johanna married Herman Toepperwein's brother Ferdinand. Adelbertha married outside the circle, but her daughter Kathinka married Paul Toepperwein, the brother of Herman and Ferdinand. Why didn't Herman Toepperwein marry a Bergmann? Because he married Jacob Luckenbach's daughter Amalie, from the Grape Creek community. Boerne Gesangverein member and cartwright Henry Wendler married Amalie's sister Pauline Luckenbach. One of their sons, Henry J. Wendler, married their niece and his cousin Adele Luckenbach. Another son, Adolph Wendler, married Paul Toepperwein's daughter, Wally Bertha Toepperwein, making their children Bergmann-Luckenbach-Toepperwein-Wendlers.

That brief example of local breeding habits, which omits such important intermingled Boerne gene stock as Dieterts, Fabras, Stendebachs, Holekamps and Theises—and more strains of Vogts—only scratches the surface of the tight-knit German community. It leaves out Boerne names that came from Sisterdale, such as the Behrs, and those that struggled to reach Meusebach's New Braunfels before coming to Boerne, such as the Monkens. Even Luckenbach founder Jacob Luckenbach eventually retired to Boerne, where he lived out his days.

Germania

One point worth noting about Boerne is that it became a German town simply because it was in a predominantly German region. It was not a planned colony like Fredericksburg or New Braunfels. It was not a land-grant necessity like Leiningen, Meerholz, Schoenburg or Castell. It was not something that grew out of the social and economic needs of neighboring farms, as did Grapetown or Luckenbach. And it was not a socialist experiment like Bettina or Tusculum: the Boerne townsite was in the hands of land investors long before Tusculum germinated, and Tusculum did not relocate to Boerne—it vaporized. Boerne was a straight-up commercial development driven by Anglo surveyor and land speculator John James.

Which leaves the question of how Boerne got such a fine German name, instead of being called Jamestown or Cibolo Crossing. The answer isn't entirely clear. Ludwig von Börne (Anglicized as Boerne) never visited the United States. Born Lob Buruch in 1786, he was a German Jew (later baptized) and a radical Frankfurt political essayist during the early phases of nineteenth-century political discontent in Germany. He was cynical: "The secret of power is the knowledge that others are more cowardly than you are." He was allegorical: "In a rolling ship, he falls who stands still, not he who moves." And he was romantic: "Nothing is permanent but change, nothing is constant but death. Every pulsation of the heart inflicts a wound, and life would be an endless bleeding, were it not for Poetry. She secures to us what Nature would deny; a golden age without rust, a spring which never fades, cloudless prosperity and eternal youth." He was popular with the Forty-Eighters and remains a respected German literary figure to this day.

We don't know enough about John James's business partner Gustav Theissen to judge whether he was a fan of Ludwig von Boerne. Theissen appears to be the "Mr. T" mentioned by renowned traveler, writer and landscape architect Frederick Law Olmstead as having the Sisterdale farm uppermost on the Guadalupe. Olmstead says that Theissen had been a member of the Frankfort parliament. We know that Theissen and Joseph Deutz opened a hardware store on the northwest corner of San Antonio's main plaza in 1856. He was a freighter; his wagons worked the Chihuahua Trail from Indianola through San Antonio to Ciudad Chihuahua. He was an organizer of the German social society and theater in San Antonio called the Casino Club, and was one of the founders of San Antonio's German-English School. He appears to have left Texas for New York during the run-up to the Civil War. It was probably he who chose the name Boerne, perhaps in consultation with the members of the Forty lingering at Tusculum. Hugo Clauss said that was the case. In all likelihood, giving the town a German name was considered a good marketing move, considering the ethnicity of most potential buyers in the area.

But a German name does not make a German town. Boerne's heritage manifested itself—and continues to do so—in its distinctly German community associations. The gesangverein, begun in 1860, continued strong under the leadership of Paul Holekamp from just after the turn of the century until 1959, then carried on until 1976 guided by Lester Lohmann.

Though there is no certain date for the founding of the Boerne Village Band, it is recognized as the oldest German band in the United States. Like the gesangverein, its origins are tied to Karl Dienger, who arrived in Boerne in 1855. By the 1880s it was flourishing; at the turn of the century the Bergmann, Stendebach, Behr, Kuhfuss and Vanderstratten families were among its ranks. Ottmar Behr, son of Ottomar von Behr, a remarkable Sisterdale pioneer, played a part in the band's early years. His grand-nephew, Dr. Kenneth Herbst, began playing in the band at age eleven and became its director, guiding it through the later years of the twentieth century into the twenty-first. The Boerne Village Band still plays a summer series of concerts in the town square. They are lovely, traditional times for family fun, oom-pah music and the occasional glass of beer.

Another German tradition that endures in Boerne is its shooting club, or schuetzenverein. Organized in 1864, its rifle range was originally on property owned by merchant and freighter William Kuhfuss on North Main Street. After a few years, the range was relocated to property behind the Phillip Manor House, a stage stop inn that still stands at 706 South Main. The club relocated at least twice more over the years as the town grew and citizens complained about the noise and risk that the range presented. Charter members of the club included Reinhold and Reinhard Kutzer, John Stendebach, Anton Bergmann, Emil Toepperwein and his brother Paul Toepperwein, Joseph Phillip (of the Phillip Manor House), William Kuhfuss and John Werner. As is often the case with German community societies, the shooting club eventually built a club house, then added a dance hall. Shooting tournaments were social and family celebrations, attended by barbecue, beer, singing and dancing. The Boerne Shooting Club still exists, out on Shooting Club Road, and is open to new members.

A turnverein is another typical German community organization. Dedicated to sports, some have gymnasia. Others, such as Boerne's, feature a bowling alley. Like the other stripes of vereins, a turnverein is primarily a social club—Boerne's original turnverein met in a building behind a saloon. It relocated to the Phillip Manor House, then to an opera house that once stood at the corner of San Antonio Street and South Main (an opera house was not necessarily about opera; Boerne's was an all-purpose community auditorium that began showing silent movies, then talkies, before becoming the Plaza Theater). In 1904 the turnverein moved to its present location; that building was replaced, only to burn down. The present Boerne Turnverein building dates to 1949 and is open to the public.

Photographs

Traffic was light enough in Boerne around 1910 that the occasional tree in the middle of the street was not a hazard to navigation. Looking north from South Main Street toward Cibolo Creek. The first building on the left is variously said to have been a general store or a saddlery. Just beyond is the Phillip Manor House. Opposite is Frank LaMotte's mansion.

William Vogt's homestead still stands just east of Plant Street. The building to the rear is his double-dogtrot connecting three cabins with a single roof.

Ludwig Fabra sits in front of Fabra's Meat Market. Built in 1857, it became a Boerne institution.

The 1860 Boerne Gesangverein. Carl Dienger (director), Hugo Clauss, Gottlieb Stephen, Henry Wendler, Herman Toepperwein, Max Falkenstein, Ferdinand Lohmann, Anton Bergmann, Albert Schluter, R. Brotze, William Vogt, Gunther Froebel, William Dietert and Henry Dietert.

William Vogt and Herman Toepperwein celebrate the fiftieth anniversary of the Boerne Gesangverein in 1910.

The Boerne Schuetzenverein circa 1891. Back row: Joe Dienger, Albert Bodeman, Paul Toepperwein, A. G. Vogt, Gus Dietert, Hugo Wendler, Adolph Luckenbach. Front row: Gus Wollschlaeger, August Theis, Eugene Laue, Henry Bickel, Ernst Beseler.

The Boerne Brass Band, progenitor of the Boerne Village Band, circa 1885. By the turn of the century the band had uniforms with brass buttons and flat-topped caps.

John James, the surveyor and land developer who laid out the Boerne townsite.

The Vollbrecht tin shop, advertising crockery and glassware on its awning, and pitching stoves and hardware on the roof sign. A tin shop was a hard-goods store and was not limited to tin. This photo does not make it easy to identify the building at 322 South Main, but it is relatively unchanged. The structure was originally built in 1879 by Henry Wendler, who sold it to his brother-in-law, Louis Vollbrecht, in the 1880s.

Crusty Louis Vollbrecht in the back of his tin shop.

Max Beseler's Metropolitan Saloon was the finest watering hole in Boerne. The ornate cherry-wood bar was installed in 1891 and moved as Beseler changed locations from 121 South Main to 141 South Main, then 143 South Main. When Prohibition was enacted in 1918, the fixture was sold. After use in an ice cream parlor for a few years, it returned to saloon duty after Prohibition was repealed. It is now in a conference room in the building now named "Boerne Center" by its most recent owners.

The crowd bustles at the Boerne depot of the San Antonio and Aransas Pass Railway. The carriage to the left, used as a taxi to take people to town, was known as an ambulance.

Members of the Boerne Cricket Team. Front row: Jack Howard, Horace Hugman, Willy Howard, J. Bright, Gerald Calrow, unknown, John Howard. Back row: King, King, Alfred Gilliat, W. Wright, Deaf Cooner, Cooper, S. Hughes, Billy Hughes, Toot Homer, unknown, unknown, unknown. Some still refer to this period as the "English Invasion."

The Dienger Building became Boerne's Public Library and served that purpose until a new library opened in 2011. It was built in 1884 and served as a grocery store with a residence upstairs. Joe Dienger's family lived and worked there in the early years when it was heated with wood stoves and had no indoor plumbing. The store stayed in the Dienger family until 1967; two years later it became the Antlers Restaurant.

The stone cottage that sat in front of the former Kendall House (O'Grady's Inn). Local legend has Robert E. Lee sleeping here. It could be true.

Built in 1879 by Charles Weyrick and sold to Fred Beissner in 1886, this building just uphill from the Phillip Manor House was once a general store, and some recall it as a saddle shop. Renovated as a private residence in 1970, it is now serves commercial uses.

August Staffel's grass-hut store and tavern was located on the northwest corner of South Main and Theissen Street. As Staffel's business interests grew he established a livery stable, a hotel and—of course—Staffel's Saloon. This building served as the office for the stable, and may also have housed Boerne's first Post Office, since Staffel served as the town's first postmaster.

The Phillip Manor House, or at least the southern wings of it. Photographs confirm the obvious—a small original structure was expanded repeatedly to achieve the present form. Over the years it has housed a hotel, an athletic club, a saloon and a dance hall. It has been known as the Cibolo Hotel, the Hotel Caroline and the Land of the Hills Hotel, and was a hardware store for a time.

Frank LaMotte purchased 1,280 acres of land from Emil Toepperwein in the 1870s and built this grand home. LaMotte sold the mansion in 1883, and over the years it has been home to many prominent local families. Rudolph Carstanjen and his family lived there from 1886 to 1905. Eventually coming to be informally known as the Mansion House, it has been a saloon and a restaurant in more recent times.

The old Boerne State Bank Building has been dressed up quite a bit over the years: the arched windows and pillars are additions made after the bank prospered. It was originally built for the Citizens State Bank in 1920; that bank merged with the Boerne State Bank during the Depression. The bank moved from this building to one of more modern design, then built the large two-story limestone bank building immediately to the north of this structure.

Rudolph Carstanjen left a mark on Boerne, in the sense that he built this building (just before his death in 1902) and a few other buildings around town (including the Carstanjen-Luckenbach house at 265 North Main). Carstanjen lived for a time in the notable house built by Frank LaMotte. But Carstanjen, who came to Boerne with a sizeable German fortune, was never especially active in the community; his buildings were investments, not businesses that he operated.

The home of Bergmann Lumber since 1969, the H. O. Adler Building was built in 1911 by Henry Oscar Adler. His family lived upstairs for many years while he operated a general store on the ground floor.

When Arnold Toepperwein and Clara Theis married, they moved into this house on Main Street. Arnold was an accomplished furniture maker known for his Ringtail Rhino logo. Their sons Gustav, Fritz and Jake were raised in this house.

Cabinet maker Henry Wendler married Pauline Luckenbach in 1865 and the couple lived in this house at 302 South Main Street. Wendler became involved in several Boerne businesses, including a general store, a saloon, a tin shop and a cabinet shop.

The John Stendebach cabin with cattle pens in front, a dogtrot log cabin in the center and a stone addition on the back. Built circa 1868, it was sold to Gustav Toepperwein in 1880.

The stone house that Gustav Toepperwein built around the turn of the century so the family could move out of the log-and-stone Stendebach cabin. In this rare snowstorm a young Toepperwein (?) stands in front of the house and a sign stuck in the snow says "buy furs."

The Boerne City Hall was once a public school built in 1911. The previous schools stood behind this building. The City of Boerne was incorporated in 1904. William Willke was the first mayor and Joe Dienger, Adolph Wendler, L. H. Schrader and L. W. King were the first aldermen.

Conventional wisdom says that the old Boerne Courthouse has had two incarnations. This is generally considered the first, built by John Stendebach in 1870. In 1909 the building was expanded to the south, adding the front of what is now called the Kendall County Historic Courthouse. After the Cass County Courthouse, it is the oldest still in use in Texas.

A close examination of the sides and rear of the building reveals not only the division between this courthouse and the newer front section, but also an apparent division between the first and second stories of the rear half. There is a difference in the shape and laying of the stone in the two stories, suggesting that the second story of the building depicted above may actually be an addition to an earlier one-story stone building. If so, Stendebach probably built both. (And there was likely a wooden courthouse that preceded the two or three stone structures.)

Hardships

It needs to be said about Boerne, and about the Hill Country generally, that not all of the German immigrants were thrilled by what they found. Storekeeper and tavern owner August Staffel was accompanied to Texas by his brother Heino and Heino's wife Adeline, who tried Boerne but ended up settling in Leon Springs. Adeline referred to her new home as "detestable Texas." The Staffels arrived in 1852 and did not have a good trip from Indianola (as Carlshaven was already being called) to New Braunfels. After chronicling the thunderstorms, broken axles and cold weather, Adeline reported that "we seldom saw a pretty view, an attractive house or a green meadow. Everything remained barren and dreary until we reached New Braunfels, which lies at the foot of some hills, with a clear stream flowing below. We did not like New Braunfels at all, and remained there only two days until a teamster took us to San Antonio."

Looking to get a business going, "Heino immediately had a desire to start a garden and seed business, and soon he located a garden by the river which rented for one-third of its crop, seed included. Soon the garden flourished so that it attracted everyone's attention. After the first four weeks, however, a drought set in which lasted two months so that most of the garden was ruined despite diligent work. Now Heino is sick [with a fever], and farewell to garden and income." The Staffels were neither the first nor the last to learn that the local climate is much more forgiving of grazing than of farming.

Adeline Staffel sounded almost optimistic when she reported that "a new town [Boerne] is to be founded between San Antonio and Fredericksburg, and everyone believes that it will be a good investment to purchase land there. Our situation has been such so far that we have saved no money, but we have no fear and need have none as ways and means can always be found for willingly working hands to learn a living." But then she allowed that "the certainty that one can establish an existence here is the only thing I like about this country. Otherwise Texas is a very miserable country, a vast prairie-like desert with only a few oases which one could call attractive.... The country, almost to Fredericksburg, where it is mountainous, is very unhealthy and no German coming here remains free of malaria fever.... Many Germans would move to Fredericksburg on account of its healthier climate, but the Indians that live there murder and plunder and nobody dares travel without adequate escort. Almost every week one hears about travelers being cruelly murdered there."

Adeline Staffel was not exactly a Texas booster, but her concern about hostile natives was not entirely misplaced. Mary Ann Schertz Becker, a Boerne innkeeper who claimed to be the first "white" child born in Boerne, used to tell tales of early days in the area. Her paternal grandparents were colonists who intended to settle in Henri Castro's Alsatian colony (though they diverted and did not homestead there); her maternal grandparents also came to Texas with the Castro colonists, but her grandfather died of cholera in Indianola and her grandmother moved to San Antonio with her mother in tow. Her mother, Segunda Ruede, married John Schertz and in 1849—before Boerne was platted—they moved to a farm three miles outside town, where Mary was born in 1854. In the florid words of a 1932 edition of the *San Antonio Express*, "Living in constant dread of the marauding bands of Indians which roamed the country, and menaced by other dangers common to the wilderness into which they had come to establish new homes, these pioneers set an example for undaunted courage. Their resolute fortitude and indomitable will has found few equals in history."

According to that same article, "When the Schertz family moved to Kendall County the hill country was filled with roving bands of hostile redskins who were a constant menace to the settlers. They made frequent raids on the sparsely settled communities, running off stock and often murdering or scalping some settler caught off his guard. When a family retired at night they had no assurance that they would not be butchered before the morning dawned."

Probing a bit deeper, it occurs that the only actual encounter with natives that Mary Becker had was once in her childhood, when she was scooping a bucket of water from Cibolo Creek. In the nearby brush she saw "an Indian buck gazing intently at her" and ran home. On another occasion her father thought he heard natives outside their cabin, so he fired his rifle through a window in the direction of the noise. Investigating later, he discovered that he had shot one of his horses. A few nights later, natives were trying to steal horses from their corral but, the story goes, Fritz Wendler was on guard in the adjacent hayloft. Wendler was so agitated by the raiders' appearance that he fell out of the hayloft. The noise and commotion scared the natives away.

Not all encounters between Germans and (usually) Comanches were so benign. In 1855 Jesse Lawhon and a ranch hand were looking for some oxen on Curry's Creek near Boerne when they were ambushed by natives. The ranch hand dashed for home and made it safely, but Lawhon endured a cat-and-mouse chase through thickets and down a steep cliff before being shot dead. Mysteriously, the ranch hand reported that one of the attackers "was a white man and the other four Indians, naked and armed with guns. The white man was dressed in dark clothes with a white hat."

It is impossible to tell whether Boerne was more peaceful in the 1850s than in the next two decades, but most local tales of conflict with natives occur in the 1860s and 1870s. This difference could stem from any of three reasons: fewer stories remain from the earliest years, when people were more intent on pioneering than on recording their lives or printing newspapers; as more settlers entered the Hill Country, the natives felt more pressure and reacted more aggressively; and when Union troops withdrew from Texas during the Civil War, West Texas natives resurged and settlers experienced renewed resistance.

In January 1862 a thick fog settled over Boerne. A man named Reinhard (his first name is lost, but he was the grandfather of John Reinhard, who served as sheriff in 1882 and judge in 1884 and who established the Walnut Grove Resort) made a business of selling firewood to local residents. That morning he asked teenager August Theis to help with chopping, splitting and loading, but father Philip Theis felt the weather was too favorable for a Comanche raid and kept his son home. Reinhard went to the woods surrounding Boerne and began his work. Henry King, who lived in the home that would become Ye Kendall Inn, received two loads of firewood from Reinhard that day, but an expected third load never arrived. That night Reinhard's wife came to King's house, crying—Reinhard had not come home.

At four o'clock in the morning, a messenger arrived from George Kendall, after whom Kendall County is named, "saying his head shepherd had been chased to the house by Indians the evening before, and a number of his sheep flocks had come home without their shepherds. He asked that we raise a party and help him make search for the missing men. Soon after day break fifteen men were in the saddle and moved out of the town toward Kendall Ranch."

At the top of the first hill above town, just east of where the Kendall County Courthouse is today, they found Reinhard's wagon and, a distance away, his body. King said, "It appeared that he was being chased by the Indians, his horses at a full run probably, when the left fore-wheel struck a stump on the roadside, breaking off the spindle and of course bringing the wagon to a stop. Then seizing his axe, his only weapon, with the idea of defending himself, he had run about fifty yards toward the town, when he was overtaken and killed. But for the fatal stump he might have escaped. He was almost home!"

Continuing on toward the Kendall ranch, "within a few hundred yards of the premises another ghostly spectacle had been discovered. Under the branches of an old oak lay the butchered body of a German lad of about sixteen years who had been in charge of a lamb flock which was herded close to the house. By him also lay the body of a dog, one of the scotch shepherd dogs of the ranch. The faithful creature had evidently been killed while attempting to protect the young shepherd and his flock."

Reaching the Kendall property, the men from Boerne learned that the head shepherd had run to the ranch house the evening before, shouting a warning of Indians. George Kendall was in the field; his wife sent the head shepherd and a helper out to look for the three flocks that were tended by hands named Schlosser, Fechler and Baptiste. Then she gathered all of her children, with her mother and Schlosser's wife, into one room in the Kendall house. Putting on her husband's overcoat and hat, she took a double-barreled shotgun and paced the front gallery, keeping guard. George Kendall returned that night and, learning of the circumstance, sent to Boerne for help.

The young man found dead under the oak tree was Fechler. Following the attackers' trail, they found the body of Baptiste face-down in a creek, four arrows in his back and his dog, Pink, standing guard. They looked all day for Schlosser, without success. Three weeks later they found his mutilated body.

It turned out that the raiders had begun their rampage on Wasp Creek, seven miles northeast of Boerne, where they intercepted farmer Louis Donop, who was riding to the creek to carry a day's rations to a man who was making shingles for him in the cypress bottoms along the creek. Donop was riding a farm horse, not nearly as fleet as the attackers' mounts, and they quickly caught him and ended his life. In one day on the outskirts of Boerne the natives—reportedly twenty-five or thirty men—had slain five settlers.

In October 1864, natives again raided Donop's widow's farm, killing and wounding horses. Three miles downstream on the Guadalupe, they stole four horses from a Mr. Helligman. John O'Grady assembled a posse and pursued, to no avail.

In July 1868, five Indians attacked eighteen-year-old Herman Stieler two miles from Comfort. He managed to defend himself with rifle and pistol, but lost the contents of his wagon to the raiders. In the spring of 1870 natives rode up to the home of John Stendebach while he was absent, terrifying his wife and children. Luckily, according to the *Boerne Star*, "all the Indians wanted was food. They grabbed the still hot boiled ham from the table and while one Indian held it in both hands, the others bit out huge chunks and chewed. They scooped up the beans and cornbread with their hands and disappeared almost as fast as they had entered. About fifteen minutes later a band of Rangers rode up, asking if any Indians had been seen. Upon relating her story, Mrs. Stendebach was told that the Indians had just murdered a family a few miles away and the Rangers were hot on their trail."

A year later, ten-year-old Clint Smith and his eight-year-old brother Jeff were kidnapped by a band of Apaches and Comanches (so the story goes) while herding sheep on their parents' farm a few miles southeast of Boerne. Their cousin, John Sansom, was a noted Texas Ranger (and a figure in Boerne's history); his company of rangers, assisted by local militia and a citizens' posse, pursued the kidnappers, but failed to catch them. Jeff Smith claimed to have been sold to Apache Chief Geronimo at some point. The boys spent five years in captivity before being returned to their families. They had some difficulty re-adjusting to their previous lives, but both married, raised children and became trail drivers, cowboys and ranchers. The Smiths also enjoyed fame on the Wild West Show circuit, and would dress up in buckskins and war bonnets well into their senior years. Their story was reduced to writing in 1927; it is full of tales of scalpings, harrowing escapes, famous Indian chiefs and the pleasures of eating raw meat with your hands. The reader comes away with the sense that the epic may have been embellished somewhat, but there is no doubt that the Smith brothers spent a remarkable five years in captivity.

BOERNE

Kendall County

In December 1859 ninety-five citizens of Kerr, Blanco and Bexar Counties drew up a petition for the creation of a new county that would include parts of the existing three. The petitioners complained that the territory where they lived was too distant from the county seats at Kerrville, Blanco and San Antonio, and that they needed a center of government somewhere in the vicinity of Sisterdale, Boerne and Comfort. The first signature on the petition was that of George Kendall, after whom the county would be named. Other familiar names appear on the petition: Wendler, Vogt, Fabra, Staffel, Herff, Theis, Bergmann, Dienger, Stendebach and more.

The Texas legislature created Kendall County on January 10, 1862, and appointed Adam Vogt, a member of the Forty and a Tusculum veteran, commissioner to oversee the organization of the county government. The voters elected Vogt to be county judge and tapped former Texas Ranger John Sansom as sheriff. To the consternation of Comfort, only Boerne and Sisterdale were far enough from the county's perimeter to qualify as county seat. In the ensuing election, Boerne prevailed over Sisterdale.

Why was the county named after George Kendall, a recent non-German arrival? His signature at the top of the petition hints at the important role he played in getting the legislature to create the new county, but there is more, for Kendall was a most remarkable man. Born in Vermont in 1809, he apprenticed with a Vermont printer and then worked for Horace Greeley in New York. Greeley was then a young printer and had not yet founded *The New Yorker*. After a brief stint with the Mobile *Alabama Register*, Kendall moved to New Orleans and co-founded the *Picayune*. There he became a successful newspaperman and a vocal proponent of the annexation of Texas. In 1841 he joined the ill-fated Texan expedition to Santa Fe and ended up imprisoned in a Mexican leper colony. He wrote more than twenty brave and fascinating letters from Mexico, and they were printed in the *Picayune*.

After Kendall's release from prison in 1842 he wrote a classic account of the expedition, then turned his interest toward advocacy of war with Mexico over the western territory. When the war began in 1846, Kendall signed up with Captain Benjamin McCulloch's company of Texas Rangers and reported from the front, gaining him accolades as the nation's first war correspondent. He reported on Winfield Scott's invasion of Vera Cruz and was wounded in the battle for Chapultepec. After the war, he wrote a well-received history of the conflict.

With his nationwide reputation as a swashbuckling journalist secure, Kendall left the day-to-day newspaper business, entering the Texas sheep industry in the early 1850s, but still writing to the *Picayune* about his experiences. He developed fine herds of Merino and Rambouillet sheep—first near New Braunfels, then on a ranch near Boerne—and promoted Texas and the Hill Country to all who read his columns. By the time he circulated the petition to form Kendall County, he was one of the most prominent and admired citizens in the region.

If George Kendall was the namesake of Kendall County, then petition co-signer and stonemason John Stendebach could be called the county's builder. He built the first county courthouse, the first county jail, the home that became Ye Kendall Inn, the Opperman house (911 South Main), the Richter house (no longer standing) and several other houses. Stendebach not only built the county jail, he operated it when he served as sheriff from 1870 to 1882. Always an investor and speculator in real estate, Stendebach was one of the people who made Boerne grow.

During the 1850s the region that became Kendall County gained a reputation as a center of German freethinking. Freethinkers were secularists committed to a rigidly rational worldview. Their lives were governed by reason, not religion, faith or tradition. Sisterdale and Comfort were especially known for their freethinking tendencies, but Boerne was not exempt from its influences. Organized religion was anathematic to freethinkers, thus when the Catholic Church sent the Reverend Emil L. J. Fleury to Boerne in 1860, he was obliged to tread carefully, despite having the support of George Kendall, John O'Grady, Joseph Phillip and local German stalwarts such as August Staffel, Karl Dienger and Casper Sultenfuss. Legend has it that St. Peter's Catholic Church sits on its hill south of Cibolo Creek because that location was outside freethinking Boerne's townsite, and thus less controversial. Or it might have been sited there because it is a splendid location for a church.

Fleury, with help from many others, built the original church by hand from limestone, completing the backbreaking task in 1867. The church still stands next to the Spanish Colonial Revival church that now dominates the St. Peter's campus, which was completed in 1923 and is modeled after San Antonio's Mission Concepcion.

In 1991 the Archbishop of San Antonio sent Reverend Anthony Cummins to Boerne to lead an expansion of the church. A controversy immediately erupted over Cummins' proposal to tear down the 1923 building and replace it with a modern structure. At about the same time, Boerne enacted its historic preservation ordinance, giving it control over changes to the church's exterior. The city maintained a prohibition on alterations to the structure until 1993, when Congress enacted the Religious Freedom Restoration Act; then the Catholic Church claimed that it was exempt from the ordinance under the terms of that law, and the battle was on. The resulting litigation eventually reached the justices at the United States Supreme Court, who found the RFRA unconstitutional. The church and the city then negotiated an agreement under which the front three sides of the 1923 structure remained intact and an addition was made to the rear.

The second church in Boerne was St. Helena's Mission, now St. Helena's Episcopal Church, which served many of the county's English families after its establishment in 1873. Services were originally held at Kuhfuss Hall (a room in the Kuhfuss Building over a saloon at 179 South Main Street; the Kuhfuss Building burned in the 1908 fire and was replaced by the present Gilliat Building). The congregation built its original frame church in 1881 and replaced it with the present stone Gothic structure in 1929.

A small group of Methodists began meeting in 1875 under the guidance of Reverend Witt. The church was reorganized with a larger congregation in 1877 by Pastor H. W. South. Like the Episcopal Church, they held services first at Kuhfuss Hall and rotated among several locations before building a church for the Boerne Methodist Church in 1879.

Given the heavy German population in Kendall County, it would seem that a Lutheran church might have been among the first to arrive, but Max Theis, grandson of pioneer Boerne wheelwright and blacksmith Philip Theis, said that when he was baptized at age six in 1903, the venue in which an itinerant Lutheran preacher performed the ceremony was a saloon across the street from the Theis house. A Lutheran congregation organized in Boerne in 1891, without an established house of worship; St. John's Lutheran Church dates to 1929.

Civil War

The year 1862 was difficult for the Hill Country. A significant element of the German community in Fredericksburg, Boerne, Sisterdale and Comfort were Unionists. The same was true among the Germans in San Antonio and Austin, though Germans in New Braunfels and East Texas tended to place their loyalty with the State of Texas before the United States.

This is not to say that Boerne—or Hill Country Germans generally—were Unionists. Their sentiments were divided (three Toepperwein brothers served in the Confederate Army, as did other Boerne citizens) but there was a tendency of the freethinkers and liberal Forty-Eighters to remain loyal to the Union and reject slavery.

In the Hill Country, German Unionism spawned insurrection. The epicenter of resistance was an organization known as the Union Loyal League; its Hill Country chapter had members scattered across the region. The league formed a private militia, talked of revolution and held secret meetings.

Oddly enough, a company of Texas State Troops was another element of Unionist insurrection in the Hill Country. Jacob Kuechler's company, based in Fredericksburg but enrolling across a wide area, was a thinly disguised German Unionist militia, and it soon came to the attention of Confederate authorities in San Antonio.

The Hill Country was under the jurisdiction of Confederate General Hamilton P. Bee, commanding the Confederate Rio Grande sub-military district from its headquarters in San

Antonio. On May 28 General Bee declared martial law in San Antonio and Bexar County. On May 30 Brigadier General Paul O. Hebert, commanding officer for the Department of Texas, extended martial law to cover the entire state. He required all white males over sixteen years of age to register with the local provost-marshal and demanded that aliens in Texas execute oaths of loyalty to Texas and the Confederacy. Seeking to clear out lingering Unionists, he directed the provosts–marshal to "order out and remove from their respective districts all disloyal persons and all persons whose presence is injurious to the interests of the country."

James M. Duff was captain and commanding officer of a company of irregular volunteers known as Texas Partisan Rangers. A Scotsman by birth, he had arrived in the United States in 1848 and had promptly enlisted in the army for a term that ended in 1854. When the Civil War began, he assembled a company of Texas volunteers that disarmed a company of Union troops during their expulsion from the state, despite protests from the federal troops that Duff was acting in contravention of the treaties reached between Texas authorities and Union General David Twiggs. Duff's volunteers morphed into Partisan Rangers and came under Confederate control.

On May 28, 1862, acting under orders from General Bee, Duff's company left Camp Bee near San Antonio and marched toward Fredericksburg. Arriving on the thirtieth, Duff formalized Bee's and Hebert's declarations of martial law as applied to Gillespie County and a portion of Kerr County, giving citizens of those districts six days to report to the provost-marshal and take the Confederate oath of allegiance. Duff prosecuted his work violently, resulting in the hanging of many suspected Unionists. One of Duff's own men described him as being "as cowardly, cold-blooded a murderer as I had ever met, even in the roaring days of the Kansas 'War.'"

Two weeks later, Duff moved his camp to Boerne, where he went through his ritual of formally declaring martial law in Kendall County and demanding loyalty oaths. He took Julius Schlickum, a local merchant and captain of a Kendall

County company of Texas State Troops, into custody on suspicion of forwarding information and communications for Unionists. For good measure, Duff imprisoned Mrs. Schlickum, too. Two days later Duff received orders to return to San Antonio and did so, leaving the Hill Country notably rattled by his visit.

The view of the Hill Country from San Antonio did not improve in July. General Bee convened a military tribunal in San Antonio to consider "all offenses accomplished or intended, which shall be injurious to the Confederate States of America, and beneficial to the United States of America." The defendants were to be the alleged Unionists rounded up by Duff and by other troops under General Bee.

Merchant and Captain Julius Schlickum of Boerne was tried in July. The charge was that "in his general deportment he is calculated to create discontent and dissatisfaction with this Government and its currency." He protested that he was not a Unionist and had taken the requisite Confederate loyalty oath.

Three witnesses appeared before the commission. Erastus Reed (then living in today's Kendall Inn) was damning: Schlickum had no sympathy for the Confederate States; while Reed knew of no particular acts that Schlickum had taken, "his general conversations has been such as would lead anyone to suppose that he was opposed to the Confederacy." Linking Schlickum to the Union Loyal League militia, he reported that Schlickum "said he knew of such an organization, but that it was for self defense. He said he knew there were over one hundred men out in the woods, said he did not belong to the organization." In a second appearance before the tribunal, Reed went further, directly accusing Schlickum of being an abolitionist.

George Kendall wasn't much help. "I never heard the accused say anything by which I could judge whether he was in favor of one Govm't or the other. I know nothing of the accused opinions on the Slavery question. I never heard anyone say that the accused was a friend to the South. I never asked anyone whether the accused was friendly to the South."

Joseph Graham said that when he visited Schlickum's store "he always appeared to be in possession of news, more favourable to the North than to the South.... When Capt. Duff's Co was up the country the accused told me that he heard he was to be arrested, asked my advice as to what he should do." It didn't help when Graham reported that "He said he might have sung some Yankee songs, but that he was drunk, and did not think it treason. I told the accused that he was accused of being an Abolitionist. He said, 'I was brought up in Europe & my views and yours differ.'"

It didn't require much evidence to be convicted of creating discontent and dissatisfaction, and Schlickum undermined his own defense by complaining that Reed and Kendall were hypocrites because they had until recently shared his Unionist sentiments. Schlickum was found guilty and sentenced to imprisonment until the war was over.

The incongruity of Schlickum—a captain of Texas State Troops—being convicted of Unionism was hardly unique. Jacob Kuechler, captain of the notorious Fredericksburg company, was already a fugitive. His second in command, Gillespie County Sheriff (and Texas State Troops Lieutenant) Philip Braubach, was under arrest and on the trial docket immediately after Schlickum.

Things did not work out as intended for Schlickum and Braubach. They escaped prison on the night of Sunday, August 2, and were never recaptured. By August 29 the tribunal worked its way around to Mrs. Schlickum, who had been arrested in Boerne more than two months earlier. It released her without trial.

A lot had happened in the Hill Country during the two months that Mrs. Schlickum had languished in jail. "In July," according to General Bee, "information was received establishing the fact that... traitors were unquestionably in arms against the Government and had assembled in the [Hill Country] counties designated, their force being variously estimated at from 100 to 500. Numerous statements were also received that these banded traitors were moving their goods and families, with large supplies of provisions, into the mountain districts, and were carrying off the property in some instances of loyal citizens, and at last, to set beyond a doubt their objects and intentions, positive intelligence was received of their having waylaid and murdered one or two well-known secession or loyal citizens."

The general appointed Captain James Duff, who had only recently returned from the Hill Country, as provost-marshal for the region and placed four companies of Texas Mounted Rifles under his control. The goals were similar to those of Duff's previous foray: declare martial law and demand oaths of allegiance upon penalty of being "treated summarily as traitors in arms." That phrase—treated summarily as traitors in arms—was loaded with meaning for a man such as Duff.

Duff's four companies were also ordered to "send out scouting parties into the mountain districts with orders to find and break up any such encampments and depots as had been reported to exist there, and to send the families and provisions back to the settlements."

The reappearance of the dreaded Captain Duff took the wind out of Unionist sails. Scores of men who had been hiding in the hills and consorting with the Unionist militia returned to their homes, bit their tongues and took loyalty oaths.

Even the hard core of the Union Loyal League's militia realized that they had gone too far. When the league's leaders heard of Duff's arrival in July, and learned of General Bee's determination to wipe out any Hill Country resistance, they decided to disband. Those who were still unwilling to swear allegiance to the Confederacy decided to flee for Mexico. They were joined by newly elected Kendall County Sheriff John Sansom.

Unbeknownst to the Unionists who rode toward the border, a company of Duff's troops followed them and caught up at the Nueces River. A firefight ensued in which nine or ten of the Germans were killed and another dozen were wounded. The remainder, including Kuechler and Sansom, managed to escape. After the battle, the Confederates shot the wounded and left their bodies unburied. For this disgrace, the affair is sometimes dubbed the "Massacre on the

Nueces." There is a monument to the dead Unionists in Comfort. Inscribed "Truer der Union," it is often incorrectly said to be the only monument in a Confederate State honoring Unionist losses.

Arrivals

Boerne might be no more than a wide spot in the road were it not for its position near the Camino Viejo and Cibolo Creek. Sitting thirty miles north of San Antonio, Boerne was a full day's ride, making it a logical layover for travelers.

From its founding through 1882, Boerne was a stop on the stage line from San Antonio to El Paso. Originally operated by Henry Skillman and financed by George Giddings, the line was extended to San Diego, California, in 1857. Services ceased during the Civil War, though Skillman continued a covert courier operation for the Confederacy from San Antonio to El Paso. In 1866 the line was turned over to a new owner and was managed by Ben Ficklin, whose successor named a Texas town after him. Benficklin, Texas, was wiped out in an 1882 flood. When the Texas and Pacific Railroad reached San Antonio in 1882, and joined the Southern Pacific Railroad in 1883, the stage line was out of business.

Though never a major cattle town, Boerne was for a time a link in the Matamoros Trail, which began at Brownsville and ran north through Santa Rosa, George West, San Antonio, Leon Springs, Boerne and Comfort, joining the Western Trail (through Bandera), in Kerrville. The Western Trail, also known as the Dodge City Trail or the Fort Griffin Trail, was blazed in 1874 and by 1879 replaced the Chisholm Trail as the major cattle route to northern markets. The introduction of barbed wire, changes in cattle breeds, cattle disease quarantines and the opening of trans-continental railroads caused the demise of the Texas cattle trails. The last known cattle drive on the Western Trail was in 1893; traffic through Boerne on the Matamoros Trail ended earlier.

It wasn't just Boerne's position on the road north and west from San Antonio that brought people to town. From 1875 to 1884, a San Antonio dentist and Boerne land investor, William Kingsbury, maintained an office in London in connection with work for the Galveston, Harrisburg and San Antonio Railway and presented himself as the Texas land and immigration agent. That was not too great a stretch, as he had served as a commissioner of the Texas Bureau of Immigration during its brief existence. He invested much of his time in London promoting Boerne, resulting in a number of English families settling there, bringing names such as King, Gilliat, Hughes, Johns, Molesworth, Upham and Whitworth to the mix.

Dr. Kingsbury had campaigned with Captain Sam Walker's company of Texas Rangers as a civilian dentist during the Mexican-American War, and was injured in battle. After the war, he practiced dentistry around southwest Texas, eventually maintaining an office in San Antonio for twenty-five years. There are some similarities between Kingsbury and Ferdinand Herff: both practiced primarily in San Antonio but were big Boerne boosters, maintained homes in Boerne and were involved in attracting the railroad to Boerne.

The Anglos brought new pursuits to Boerne—Alfred Gilliat was one of the members of Boerne's 1886 Cricket Team—with an impact that lasted well into the twentieth century. After retiring from the British military, William Glynn Turquand sailed for Texas around 1870 and purchased a ranch in northern Bexar County and southern Kendall County. An avid polo player, Turquand brought polo equipage with him and started training horses. Locals who had grown up punching cattle found themselves training polo ponies and learning the game. A level pasture along today's Upper Balcones Road, just into Kendall County, became the playing field where Turquand assembled the Boerne Polo Team. By the early 1880s polo had spread through the cavalry units manning frontier outposts, and teams began to spring up throughout the West.

In 1878 William G. "Willy" Hughes was living about four miles west of Boerne, where he had bought 160 acres for $225 to start a sheep operation. Hughes expanded and developed his ranch and his herd of sheep. Cousin James Hughes, who had arrived in the United States in 1874 and had become active in the horse and cattle trade, visited in 1879. James and Willy teamed up to crossbreed mustangs and cow ponies, but James's interest turned to New Mexico, and he moved on.

The tales of Texas that Willy sent back to England induced his brothers Harry (known as "Doc") and Gerard ("Chico") to join him in Boerne. The three bothers became partners in ranching and raising their cow pony-mustang mix.

Then Hughes' parents, sister and grandmother emigrated to Tennessee. When Willy's father Hastings arrived in Boerne for a visit in 1879, accompanied by Willy's cousin Robert Hobson, the topic of polo ponies came up, and it seemed that the Hughes' frontier crossbreed horses might be perfect for the game. The three men soon found themselves in the polo pony business. Bob began shipping his best stock to New York, and the reputation of the Texas polo pony began to spread.

In 1882 Willy's sister Madge visited Boerne. She arrived to discover that her brothers' accommodations consisted of a nine-by-twelve foot thatched-roof shanty, a large tent and a rickety board kitchen that would serve as her bedroom. The kitchen's thatch roof leaked, turning the dirt floor into mud. Madge stayed five weeks, then returned to Tennessee.

The Hughes Ranch outside Boerne became an equestrian training ground where the family transformed cow ponies into polo ponies in a matter of weeks, then shipped them east. Hastings Hughes relocated to New York to enter the wine importing business; Willie and Robert used the connection to their advantage. When one load of ponies landed in New York, Hastings met them at the dock—decked out in proper English riding regalia—and herded them through the financial district and up Fifth Avenue to their destination.

Though polo remained a passion for Willy Hughes, it would be unfair to restrict his memory to that topic. He eventually built his 160-acre ranch into a seven-thousand-acre spread and leased another fifteen thousand acres. In addition to his polo ponies, he bred fine Angora goats, Arabian horses and other champion livestock. He was a violinist with enough talent to stand before an audience at the Boerne Opera House, and a businessman with enough initiative to found and operate a stage line between Boerne and Bandera.

Cecil "Digger" Smith began playing polo in 1924 and for 26 years was a ten-goal player, the sport's highest ranking; only twenty American-born players have achieved that status. In his obituary, the *New York Times* called Smith "perhaps the greatest player in the history of a game more than 2,000 years old." Smith was a cowpuncher from Plano until age twenty, when he went to work for a San Antonio horse trader who also trained polo ponies. He picked up the sport and became a prominent trainer and player. Most of his ponies were shipped to California; the ones that didn't sell there went to Long Island. Not only was he a figure in the international polo leagues, but he found himself playing in California with the likes of Will Rogers, Darryl Zanuk and Walt Disney. Smith moved to Boerne in 1966, retiring from the tour and concentrating on training polo ponies. He died in 1999.

A century earlier, Boerne was concerned with things more mundane than polo, such as connecting to the outside world. The telegraph reached town in 1883. Eugene Laue was the first operator for Western Union, operating out of the Staffel Building.

The significance of the telegraph was eclipsed by the arrival of the San Antonio and Aransas Pass Railway. Originally chartered to cover the 135 miles between the Texas Gulf Coast and San Antonio, it extended its tracks to Boerne and Kerrville in 1887. Built by a group of San Antonio promoters, and aided by civic-minded Boerne boosters such as Ferdinand Herff and William Kingsbury, the railroad brought not only freight and commerce—it brought visitors. In the summer, residents on the sweltering, mosquito-infested Gulf Coast could escape to the Hill Country. In the winter, Hill Country residents could seek warmer weather to the south.

The railroad built a depot at the top of cleverly named Depot Road (today's Rosewood Avenue), where Eugene Laue served as station agent and telegraph operator.

The first trip of the SA&AP to Boerne was an affair privately arranged on Saturday, March 12, 1887, for about fifty San Antonio and Boerne dignitaries including the Herff family, Eugene Staffel, Eugene Laue and Sarah Reed. The following Friday the first public train, carrying a crowd that included a reporter from the *San Antonio Daily Express*, pulled into the station. A group of Boerne citizens headed by the good Doctor Kingsbury greeted the new arrivals. "We welcome you today," Kingsbury said, "not only because you bring the iron horse of commerce harnessed with iron traces, but because it will give you an opportunity to breathe our pure air and see our picturesque country, dotted with little mountains, interspersed with valleys as fertile as the famed Scotia. We have a climate and a country here unsurpassed; in fact, unapproached by any in the broad state of Texas—and that means by any on the face of the earth."

The reporter from the *Daily Express* wrote that "the sun was just dropping behind a bank of beautiful red over the hill that girds the city on the west when the engine began to puff and paw on its return trip. Handkerchiefs fluttered out the windows, and were responded to by flapping linen strewn along the track as far as the eye could see and reaching back to the centre of the town. There was no business in the village during the day. Stores and workshops were closed and the front doors of residences were standing wide open. The town was on a frolic and is liable to keep it up for a day or two longer."

Boerne became known as a health resort in the late nineteenth century. Dr. Ernst Kapp had operated a hydrotherapy institute and spa known as Badenthal in Sisterdale since the 1850s. In 1885 John Reinhard and his wife opened a boarding house in Walnut Grove, five miles from Boerne on Sisterdale Road. The boarding house expanded into cottages, tennis courts and stables. By the turn of the century it was a noted tourist attraction.

According to a San Antonio newspaper, "The burg is principally noted for the unlimited quantity and excellent quality of its ozone, whatever that is, its surpassing beauty, its beer (San Antonio variety), its public spirited citizens, pretty girls, good hotels [and] for being the country home of the Herff family." The article had a few more words to say about one of "the noted institutions of Boerne, and that is the keno room. Cards are three for a quarter, and the game is played in the same old way. All sit around a rough pine table deeply absorbed in the numbers called out by the dealer, until one man yells 'keno,' and the others say 'Oh, hell!' only they say it in German and it don't sound so bad—to English ears it's almost polite."

Boerne had several hotels in its early days. The one most often thought of is the Kendall Inn, but that was not the same property that is today called Ye Kendall Inn. The original Kendall Inn was on the east side of South Main Street, just south of Cibolo Creek. Built by John G. O'Grady in 1859, it was also known as the Kendall House or the O'Grady Inn. O'Grady had been the quartermaster at Fort McKavett before coming to Boerne; he served as Boerne's second postmaster beginning in 1861, following August Staffel. (Having a post office was a sign of municipal distinction then, and serving as postmaster was considered an honor.) The inn is gone now, replaced by a residence long ago. A small stone cottage still stands near the front of the property, part of the original O'Grady Inn complex. Legend has it that Robert E. Lee slept in that cottage while traveling on the military road. That can't be proven, but it is the sort of story that every small town should have. (And it is certain that Lee traveled through Boerne more than once as an officer of the United States Army based in San Antonio.)

The building that is today called Ye Kendall Inn was originally a private residence of smaller proportions. John Stendebach built the center segment in 1859 as a home for Erastus and Sarah Reed, who later leased to Henry Chipman, then sold the building in 1869 to Colonel Henry King and his wife, Jean Adams King. In 1878, as Boerne began to be known as a health resort, a pair of Dallas investors bought the King home, added two long wings to the building and named it the Boerne Hotel. The Boerne Hotel served for a time as a stage stop inn and was the most substantial lodging house in town. It wasn't until 1909, when the building was bought by San Antonio physician H. J. Barnitz, that it was given the faux English name Ye Kendall Inn. By then O'Grady's original Kendall Inn was but a memory.

August Vogt, known as "A. G." came to Boerne from Seguin in 1856 as an infant. He and Pauline Pfeiffer married in Boerne in 1876 and bore twelve children. In 1884 the couple bought a lot on Main Street where they constructed their home. While A. G. Vogt tended to his store, Pauline began taking in boarders; as that business thrived—and the Vogt family grew—they expanded their residence into a boarding house for summer visitors. A week's room and board at the Vogt House cost $4.50 at the turn of the century. The Vogt House is gone now, replaced by the large, two-story limestone building at Main and Rosewood (of recent construction) that was once the Boerne State Bank and has recently been titled "Boerne Center" by its latest owners.

The Becker House stood across Main Street from the Vogt House. It was run by Mary Ann Schertz Becker, whose stories of Indian depredations I recounted earlier. Though the family lived on a ranch outside town, father John Schertz bought two ten-acre lots in Boerne when it was founded, and built a cabin there. John Schertz died young; his widow and children moved into town, then built a lodging house at the front of their lots. Opened in 1896, the Becker House expanded from three to nine to fifteen rooms as business grew. Originally a transient hotel, then catering to drummers (traveling salesmen), the operation became oriented toward longer-term summer boarders attracted to Boerne's healthy climate. Mrs. Becker served her guests turkey dinner every Monday. The southeast corner of Rosewood and Main, where the Becker House stood, now boasts a gasoline station.

We have mentioned the Phillip Manor House, which once hosted the Boerne Schuetzenverein. It was probably constructed shortly after the Civil War, and one glance at the building (at 706 South Main) reveals that it experienced a series of additions over the years. It was originally the home of Joseph V. Phillip, who made his fortune in shingle-making and construction. After his death in 1887 his son—also Joseph Phillip—turned it into a hotel.

The Phillip Manor House, the Kendall Inn (O'Grady House) and the Boerne Hotel (Ye Kendall Inn) were the premium stops in Boerne, though the family boarding houses—notably Becker and Vogt—provided good, clean lodging and family meals. In its early days, Boerne also had a St. James Hotel and a Sunset Hotel, but these have passed into the mists of time, leaving hardly a trace.

In the 1890s, and again after the First World War, Boerne's healthy climate attracted the infirm. Dr. Ferdinand Herff played a significant part in this phase of Boerne's history, backing the construction of St. Mary's Sanitarium on what is today an empty tract across from St. Helena's Episcopal Church on North Main Street (the site of Boerne's future civic campus, with Boerne's new Patrick Heath Public Library to the rear). Opened in 1896, the sanitarium was operated by the Sisters of the Incarnate Word and was affiliated with San Antonio's Santa Rosa Hospital, in which Dr. Herff was also active. These were the years of tuberculosis, and the sanitarium afforded patients life in an atmosphere believed to be more healthful than San Antonio or the Gulf Coast. The sanitarium expanded from twenty beds to fifty and treated hundreds of victims of the "White Plague" before being destroyed in 1924.

The end of the First World War brought a surge in pulmonary patients, due to both tuberculosis and gas attacks on soldiers during the war. In 1919 local physician W. E. Wright opened a sanitarium east of Main Street on Ryan Street, where it intersects Hilltop Drive. Wright's Sanitarium was composed of about fifteen four-bed cottages; it housed and treated veterans under a government contract. At times its patient load was as great as 150 veterans, with those that could not be accommodated in the cottages being treated at St. Mary's Sanitarium.

At about the same time, Emilie Lex opened a smaller sanitarium in her family home on Johns Road. Family, patients and visitors would dine together at the Lex table. The facility provided general medical care, and did not specialize in tuberculars. Mrs. Lex was a respected midwife. There was no resident physician, but doctors from Boerne could attend the handful of patients that stayed there. These were the days before antibiotics, and treatment was crude by modern standards. Buckets of ice might be carried into a room to cool it for a patient with a fever. Surgery was risky—anesthetizing the patient involved the dangerous application of ether or chloroform, and control of infection was crude.

At one point, Mrs. Lex converted two rooms of her home into operating rooms for Boerne's Dr. John F. Nooe. After getting his medical degree in Galveston and serving his internship in New York, Nooe came to Boerne, where he quickly became a prominent member of the community. He was especially known for delivering babies, but he also kept tuberculosis patients at the Lex Sanitarium and in another small facility maintained by Fritz and Juliana Adler at their home on Adler Road. A four-room addition to the southeast corner of the Adler home was originally used for borders, then redirected to health care. The wood-frame rooming addition to the stone house—known as Adler House to boarders and Winona Home to Dr. Nooe's patients—is gone now.

Not all Boerne citizens were pleased that their town had become a magnet for tuberculars and sick veterans, preferring the days when tourists would come for the healthy air, stay a few days or weeks and leave their money behind. Some blamed Drs. Herff, Nooe and Wright for the influx of the sickly, and took a dim view of the charitable works of St. Mary's Sanitarium. As the impact of tuberculosis lessened, as war veterans were processed out of the sanitariums, and as the Veterans Administration opened hospitals for their care, the demand for Boerne's health facilities diminished. All of the sanitariums were closed by 1930.

Later Years

Boerne never became an industrial or transportation hub. Its status as county seat ensured a certain amount of commerce, but no other force drove its economy.

Electricity came to Boerne in 1904, and the town incorporated as a municipality in 1909. A fire had destroyed significant parts of downtown the year before, and a few years later another downtown fire broke out. It seems as if almost every small town suffered fires of this sort—usually due to boiler explosions or primitive electrical wiring—and Boerne was not exempt. The bright side of the fires was that they sparked a small boom in construction; many of today's stone or brick buildings downtown date to this period.

The original Boerne town plat didn't lay out or name many streets. Instead, most of the town (except the strip between today's Blanco Road and East San Antonio Avenue) were either large, multi-acre town lots or forty-acre outlots, undivided by roads. As large lots were split and streets emerged, roads were often named after founders or local families: Theissen Street, Herff Street, Lohmann Street, Schleicher Street and so forth. Another popular naming convention was more colloquial: School Street goes by the school; Plant Street passed the ice plant on River Road; Depot Road went to the railroad depot; Blanco Road went to Blanco and Bandera Road went to Bandera. In a similar vein, Johns Road goes by the Johns family home and Adler Road goes by the Adler family's property. But San Antonio Avenue does not go to San Antonio.

The first newspaper in Boerne was the *Union Land Register*, begun in 1875 by C. G. Vogel, a land developer who created the town of Kendalia. Around 1888, Frederick W. Schweppe, prominent lawyer and judge, acquired the paper and renamed it the *Boerne Advance.* That paper folded when Schweppe retired. In 1890, John Guthrie, formerly editor of the *Bandera Bugle*, moved to Boerne and established the *Boerne Post*, which he published until he died in 1906. That year L. N. Cook acquired the *Boerne Post* and began the *Boerne Star*.

In 1907 William Gammon Davis watched in dismay as his cotton crop near Groesbeck was destroyed by boll weevils. That was bad enough, but in the fall of that year Limestone County exercised its local option to become a dry county. Davis moved to Boerne and bought the local papers, consolidating them into the *Boerne Star*. The *Star's* operations passed from father to son to grandson over seventy years; since 1978 it has changed ownership outside the family several times.

The first decade of the twentieth century was probably the peak of agricultural production for Kendall County. Cotton was king; there were perhaps a dozen cotton gins in the county. The shell of one still stands in Sisterdale.

The first Kendall County Fair took place in 1906 at the opera house downtown. Seven years later the Kendall County Fair Association formally organized; the Herff family donated land for the county fairgrounds.

The early decades of the twentieth century also saw the birth of the semi-professional Boerne White Sox baseball team. Baseball was popular in the first years of the century, and by 1912 the team had a name and uniforms. The semi-pro Hill Country League formed in the 1920s, then reorganized itself into the Mountain League in the 1930s. Boerne, Bandera, Comfort, Kerrville, Fredericksburg, Mason, Blanco and Llano battled it out on the diamond before crowds that sometimes reached two thousand fans. Interest in semi-pro ball faded with the advent of television in the 1950s, and continued to dwindle. In 1973 the Boerne White Sox hung up their gloves.

It is odd how drugstores became community centers during—and memorable places from—the early twentieth century. In Boerne, that institution was originally Kuhlmann's Apothecary, established by William Kuhlmann around 1880 at 195 South Main Street. Just after the turn of the century William Willke, who would become Boerne's mayor in 1909, acquired the building and business. Arthur Fabra bought the business in 1923, and hired Max Theis to manage it for him. The business changed hands several more times over the years. It was known as the Roberts Drug Store until 1971. The building still stands, now an antique shop.

From 1904 to 1920 there was another drug store in town: Levyson's, in the Rud Carstanjen building immediately south of town square. Albert Levyson moved his wife and son Sidney to Boerne from Shiner. Mrs. Levyson was of German birth, but they were the only Jewish family in town, which was not entirely comfortable—even though Sidney enrolled in the Holy Angels Academy operated by the Sisters of the Incarnate Word, next door to their St. Mary's Sanitarium.

Sidney worked for the *Boerne Star* and aspired to be a journalist, but his father insisted that he go into the family business; he got his degree in pharmacy from the University of Texas at Galveston, then returned to Boerne. When the Levyson family drugstore closed, he worked briefly in San Antonio. In 1920 Sidney was diagnosed with Hansen's Disease, dreaded then as leprosy. The disease was so emotionally charged in that era that Sidney Levyson changed his name to Stanley Stein when he was admitted to the U. S. Leprosarium in Carville, Louisiana. The disease blinded him in 1937, but did not stop him from founding a bi-monthly magazine named the *Sixty-Six Star* that advocated the rights of victims of the disease. Now called simply *The Star*, it is still widely read and influential. Because of Levyson's crusading efforts, the name of the facility was changed to the U. S. Public Health Service Hospital (now the National Hansen's Disease Programs) and the government dropped the name leprosy in favor of Hansen's Disease. In 1963 Levyson published his noted autobiography, *Alone No Longer*, "the story of a man who refused to be one of the living dead." Levyson died in

1967 after changing the world in his own small but important way.

After the First World War, the resort and healthy air businesses declined and Boerne began to slide into stagnation. A municipal water system was built in 1927; it took another twenty years for sewer and gas utilities to be installed.

As the nation slipped into depression in the 1930s, so did Boerne, already staggering from the effects of a boll weevil infestation in 1925. In some ways Boerne resurged during the Second World War, deriving activity from the military boom in San Antonio, but the county lost population as tourism and farming diminished. Ranching—less labor intensive and less dependent upon the vagaries of nature—increasingly replaced farming. Many veterans who went off to war never returned. The war changed the United States, stripping its naivete. Interest in local traditions—the gesangverein, schuetzenverein, turnverein and band—cooled.

Boerne was a family-oriented small county seat. The liberal and secular views of the town's founders gradually changed into a conservative, religious lifestyle.

Bergesfest—an all-purpose good time held annually on Fathers' Day Weekend—was created by the Chamber of Commerce in 1967 to draw attention and visitors to Boerne. Edgar Voges won a contest to name the event; Bergesfest means Mountain Festival or, for local audiences, Hill Country Festival. In those days there were quite a few empty storefronts on Main Street, and the festival was a welcome shot in the arm for Boerne. The Chamber—in partnership with the Boerne Visitors Center—remains an active civic booster, hosting or attracting a number of annual events, quite a few of which are oriented toward people who like to admire automobiles.

Construction of Interstate 10 in the 1960s brought more traffic and more people to the Boerne area, and made it more accessible to San Antonio and Houston. The Texas economy suffered mightily with the end of the 1980s oil boom. As the state began to recover, so did Boerne. And as San Antonio grew to the north, ripples spread into the Hill Country. The north side of San Antonio attracted USAA, the University of

Texas at San Antonio and the San Antonio Medical Center, followed by Sea World, Fiesta Texas, La Canterra and a spate of upscale resort hotels.

In the last couple of decades Boerne's historic downtown has become something of a tourist attraction, but Boerne is too close to San Antonio and too far from Austin or Houston to match Fredericksburg in that department, which may not be all bad.

Beginning in the 1980s, Boerne embarked on a careful and thoughtful approach to municipal finance, capital improvement programs and city planning. A large bond issue funded quality of life improvements such as walking trails, sidewalks, parks, and improvements along Cibolo Creek. To protect its cultural, historic and natural assets, Boerne has established a historic preservation district and adopted ordinances protecting trees and entry corridor esthetics. The work continues.

The onion dome on the bandstand in the town square has become an iconic image for Boerne, but in fact dates only to the 1980s, when it was purchased and installed by the Boerne Optimist Club.

The Cibolo Nature Center, established by Carolyn Chipman Evans, a great-great-great-granddaughter of Ferdinand Herff, has grown from an ambitious idea to a world-class facility rapidly gaining national recognition.

Jim Keeter, a local landscape architect, improved the looks of Boerne's Main Street crossing at Cibolo Creek by bringing in and renovating not one, but two railroad depot buildings. Beware, though—neither was the Boerne depot for the San Antonio and Aransas Pass Railway (though two old Boerne depot buildings stand at a new locations in Boerne), and the site of the Boerne depot was nowhere near that location. It was where Rosewood Avenue (formerly Depot Road) crosses the old railroad right of way on top of the hill east of downtown.

That right of way is now the Old Number 9 walking path, a community amenity built by the city at the urging of several people, particularly Paul Barwick and Carolyn Chipman Evans. It is a welcome addition to the town, but it does not follow the tracks of the Old Number 9 Railroad. That is because there was no Old Number 9 Railroad.

Old Number 9 was Texas Highway 9, thus designated in 1917 and running from Corpus Christi through San Antonio, Boerne and Fredericksburg to Amarillo and beyond (it was to be part of a highway from the Gulf of Mexico to Puget Sound). It was Main Street through Boerne, then followed Spanish Pass Road (now a dead end) into Welfare, Waring and toward Comfort. U. S. Highway 87 (which took a more westerly route from Leon Springs to Boerne, Comfort and Fredericksburg), replaced State Highway 9, causing Welfare, Waring, Grapetown and Bankersmith to atrophy.

The pathway called the Old Number 9 in Boerne is in fact the bed of the San Antonio & Aransas Pass Railway, which had little relation to Highway 9. History is forgiving, though, and will surely overlook this small error. Besides, "Old Number 9" would have been a great name for a railroad.

Epilogue

I began this book by telling you of our run-down farm, and of my curiosity about its history. Let me tell you what I learned—you will encounter some familiar names.

Johann Franz Stendebach was a farmer, a stone mason and—like many on the Texas frontier—a land speculator. Born in Prussia in 1826, he emigrated to Texas in 1852, settling initially in San Antonio with his father Johannes, his mother Catherine and his sister Maria, all of whom had arrived a few months earlier. Father Johannes invested in several San Antonio properties, including a piece of land bounded by Nacogdoches, Bowie and Crockett Streets—adjacent to the Alamo, where the Crockett Hotel stands today.

In San Antonio, Johann Franz changed his name to John Frank Stendebach. Soon he met and married eighteen-year-old Anna Katharina Nickel, who had also come to Texas from Prussia with her parents. Seeking their own destiny, the couple homesteaded 160 acres on Honey Creek in western Comal County, about ten miles northeast of Boerne. Their first child, William Peter, was born in November and would also become a stone mason. They would have nine more children. Three died in early childhood. Two sons (in addition to William Peter) and four daughters survived. Carolina, one of the daughters, would marry Martin Monken, the son of Bernard Monken, whose family's travails from Indianola to New Braunfels we tracked earlier.

Stendebach stood out locally. He was one of the signatories on the 1852 petition that created Kendall County, served as sheriff in 1870 and was a charter member of the Boerne Schuetzenverein. As I mentioned earlier, he was the man who built much of Boerne.

Like his father, John Stendebach believed in investing in land, purchasing more than a dozen properties over the years. In August 1868 he bought two Boerne outlots containing eighty acres for $350. We paid considerably more for 23 of those acres in 2002.

Stendebach went to work clearing the land and built a two-room dogtrot cabin with livestock pens on the front. One room had a fireplace, and there was a loft above the other room where the children probably slept. Later he built a stone addition across the back of the cabin, closing in the dogtrot and creating two more rooms. It was in this cabin that Anna Stendebach was confronted by raiding natives who helped themselves to ham and beans. The cabin still stands today; I have stood in the small room with a hearth, trying to imagine the moment.

The Stendebachs lived on their Boerne farm for eleven years, selling it to Friedrich Hofheinz in August 1879. Over John and Anna's signature is the statement that the land is "our present homestead." Like Stendebach, Hofheinz dealt in property; this was only one of several transactions between the two men over the years. In November of 1880, Hofheinz re-sold the land, almost certainly without ever occupying it. The buyer was forty-four-year-old Gustav Adolph Toepperwein.

I have mentioned the Toepperwein family before; they first settled along Grape Creek before moving to Boerne and Leon Springs. Gustav married Charlotte Lohmann and they had four children: Emma Marie, Arnold Sophus, Alma Charlotte and Hedwig Wilhelmina. Emma, the oldest, was twelve when the Toepperweins moved into the dogtrot cabin built by Stendebach. Arnold, who became a fine furniture maker known for the "Ringtail Rhino" logo that he carved into the back of his pieces, married Clara Theis (granddaughter of Philip Theis) in the cabin; they draped the walls with unbleached muslin and lit candles for the ceremony.

Gustav, who operated a general store opposite Boerne's town square and farmed on the land he bought from John Stendebach, was one of a well-known extended family of Toepperweins. Like John Stendebach, Gustav's brothers Emil and Paul were charter members of the Boerne Schuetzenverein. Emil was a gunsmith; his son Adolph "Ad" Toepperwein became a famous trick-shot artist in Wild West Shows, as did Ad's wife Elizabeth Servaty "Plinky" Toepperwein.

Paul Toepperwein was Boerne's first public schoolteacher. Brother Herman (who married Amalie Luckenbach) was a charter member of the first Boerne Gesangverein, organized by Carl Dienger and Hugo Clauss. He was the first Kendall County Attorney. Herman, Amalie and his parents were buried on his farm near Leon Springs; the family plot is now within the Dominion subdivision.

Gustav's cabinetmaker son Arnold moved into Boerne when he married Clara Theis. Their son Fritz married Emilie Mathieson, who hailed from California. Fritz and Emilie became interested in handicraft printing. Using an old hand-set press that had been rescued from the Comal River during the Civil War, they turned out a series of children's books illustrated with Emilie's hand-made block prints. The books, with names such as *Little Miss Crinoline* and *Chinto, the Chaparral Cock*, are personal, almost intimate in the obvious care and love put into each hand-made volume.

After a time Gustav and Charlotte were able to build a stone farmhouse measuring just twenty-two feet square. Old photos show a one and one-half story cottage with massive posts holding up a front porch. The old dogtrot cabin was converted to a barn. A nearby building constructed of sand brick with lime mortar housed farm hands. Water came from a sixty-foot-deep hand-dug well lined with stones.

Gustav Toepperwein died in 1915. Charlotte lived much longer, passing away in 1935. They are both buried in the Boerne cemetery, just yards from John and Anna Stendebach's graves. In 1940, Emma Toepperwein, acting as executrix of her mother's estate, sold the farm to Herbert and Lottie Kohls. The place had run down, and the Kohls set about fixing it up. They had a new well drilled to ninety feet and erected a Chicago Aermotor windmill that pumped water into a tank mounted on high cedar posts. The Kohls built a new farmhouse. It measured only about eight hundred square feet, but a later expansion added another ten-by-twelve space to the living room. The farmhouse had indoor plumbing—an amenity lacking in the old Toepperwein house. Herbert Kohls tore down most of the Toepperwein residence and used the stone to build a dairy barn. He kept part of one stone room, though, and converted it to a smokehouse. When they got electricity, he installed a submersible pump in the Toepperwein well but left the windmill spinning in the wind above.

Herbert Kohls married well. Lottie was the granddaughter of Sisterdale's remarkable Ottomar von Behr; her son Charles Kohls still lives in von Behr's stone house on the Guadalupe River outside Sisterdale. The Kohls ran a dairy farm on their property until Herbert's death in 1971 at age sixty-six. Lottie outlived Herbert, dying in the little farmhouse in 2000 at age ninety-two.

In the autumn of 2002, my wife Jeanne and I drove by the dilapidated gate of Lottie's farm. A For Sale sign was cocked at an angle near the drive. The place looked deserted, abandoned, but we decided to call the phone number on the sign. Soon we were the fourth family entrusted with the old farm and its log cabin, windmill, smoke house, dairy barn, and tiny cottage.

A year or so after we bought the place I was walking in one of the pastures at sundown. I happened to glance at a rock and saw the word "EPPER" carved into it. For all my research, I had never come across that name. I resolved to get over to the county courthouse and do some digging. I never got around to the research, because I took Jeanne out to meet my friend Epper. It was evening, and the light was low and flat across the rock. Now I could see all the letters: G. A. Toepperwein. A handshake across the generations. Pleased to meet you.

Acknowledgments

I was motivated to undertake this task by the number of locals and visitors who came into my now-closed bookstore, Mockingbird Books, asking for a history of Boerne. Though there were still copies of Garland Perry's *Historic Images of Boerne and Kendall County* available at the Boerne Public Library, I had been unable to get any to stock in my store. And *Historic Images*, as excellent as it is, is not suited for every reader. Before I knew it, I was deep into Hill Country history.

Garland Perry's prodigious efforts to record Boerne's history did more than lay the groundwork for my task. The level of detail in his book is nothing short of astounding.

Colonel Bettie Edmonds is the backbone of a local effort to preserve Boerne's history. Her brief history of Boerne is still available, and you can find a copy at the Boerne Area Historical Preservation Society's headquarters. She has worked hard to document Boerne, and she kindly agreed to review this book's manuscript.

The many volunteers at the BAHPS who support Col. Edmonds have been an invaluable help, kindly permitting me to rummage through the society's immaculate files. For that matter, many thanks to the BAHPS itself, which maintains the archives and provided many of the photos for this book.

There is also a fine collection of historical and genealogical archives at Boerne's Patrick Heath Public Library. Many thanks to the library for all sorts of things, including the archives. The library staff have gone to a lot of trouble to accommodate my research, and have remained calm through the worst of it.

Historian, author and gentleman Ed Mergele has more history in his head than I have on my bookshelves. I am inspired by his comprehensive knowledge and enduring curiosity. And I am thankful that he agreed to review my manuscript before I put it before the public.

Charles Kohls, Frances Kohls, Georgeanna (Stendebach Monken) Dillon and Kenneth Toepperwein have graciously shared information about their ancestors with me. That has been important not only to this book, but also to my personal quest to understand the history of our farm.

All of the staff at the Kendall County Clerk's Office were gracious and understanding as I dug through their most ancient records, muttering and pulling my hair. It is always a pleasure to work in a well-organized, professionally managed clerk's office.

There is no point in singling out my wife Jeanne Buchanan for thanks on this particular project, as she deserves (and I hope gets) thanks for darn near everything I do. Nonetheless, thanks, Jeanne. You are the reason.

Selected Bibliography

Adam, Kathryn L. "Foreign Visionaries in the Texas Hill Country: Early German Settlers in the Kendall County Area, 1847-1900." Master's thesis, Texas Woman's University, 1979.

Anonymous. "Die Lateinische Farm," *Deutsch-Texanische Monatshefte*, II: 238 (1896).

Anonymous. *A Pioneer Family History, The Weitz Family in Texas 1852 – 1922; The First Stendebachs in Texas 1852 – 1961.* n.p., ?

Barr, Alwyn. "Records of the Confederate Military Commission in San Antonio, July 2 – October 10, 1862," *Southwestern Historical Quarterly* 70: 93 and 289 (1966) and 623 (1967), 71: 247 (1967), 73: 83 and 243 (1969).

Benjamin, Gilbert Giddings. *The Germans in Texas.* Austin: Jenkins Publishing Co., 1974.

Biesele, Rudolph Leopold. *The History of the German Settlements in Texas 1831-1861.* Austin: Von Boeckmann-Jones, 1930. Reprint, Austin: Eakin Press, 1987.

Boerne Area Historical Preservation Society. *The Journey to Boerne, Finding and Making a New Home.* n.p., 1999.

Boerne Area Historical Preservation Society. Vertical Files and Records. Boerne, Texas.

Chipman, Donald E. *Spanish Texas 1519 – 1821.* Austin: University of Texas Press, 1992.

Clauss, C. Hugo. "Aus der Vergangenheit der Ansiedlung Boerne," *Deutsche-Texanische Monatshefte*, 7: 308 (1902).

Clauss, C. Hugo. "Boerne und das Cibolo-Thal in Kendall County," *Jahrbuch fuer Texas*, 29 (1882).

Confederate States Army. *Proceedings of Confederate Military Commission Convened at San Antonio, Texas, 1862.* Texas State Library and Archives Commission, Austin.

Copeland, Fayette. *Kendall of the Picayune.* Norman: University of Oklahoma Press, 1997.

De la Teja, Jesus. *San Antonio de Bexar, A Community on New Spain's Northern Frontier.* Albuquerque: University of New Mexico Press, 1995.

Dielmann, Henry B. "Dr. Ferdinand Herff, Pioneer Physician and Surgeon." *Southwestern Historical Quarterly* 57: 268 (1954).

Edmonds, Bettie. *The Journey to Boerne: Finding and Making a New Home.* Boerne: Boerne Area Historical Preservation Society, 1997.

Elliott, Claude. "Union Sentiment in Texas, 1861-1865," *Southwestern Historical Quarterly,* 50: 449 (1947).

Genealogical Society of Kendall County. Vertical files and records. Boerne, Texas.

Glenn, Frankie Davis. *Capt'n John, Story of a Texas Ranger.* Austin: Nortex Press, 1991.

Gray, Edith A., comp. *Recollections of Boerne and Kendall County.* Boerne: n.p., 1999.

Gray, Edith A., comp. *Recollections of Boerne and Kendall County—Family Histories.* Boerne: n.p., 2003.

Herff, Ferdinand Peter. *The Doctors Herff: A Three-Generation Memoir.* Edited by Laura L. Barber. San Antonio: Trinity University Press, 1973.

Jacoby, Susan. *Freethinkers: a History of American Secularism.* New York: Henry Holt and Co. 2004.

Kaufmann, Wilhelm. *Die Deutschen im der amerikanischen Burgerkriege.* Munich: R. Oldenbourg, 1911.

Kendall County Clerk. Records. Boerne, Texas.

Kendall County District Clerk. Records. Boerne, Texas.

Kendall County Historical Commission. *A History of Kendall County, Texas: Rivers Ranches, Railroads, Recreation.* Dallas: Taylor Publishing Co., 1984.

La Vere, David. *The Texas Indians.* College Station: Texas A&M University Press, 2004.

Lich, Glen E. *The German Texans.* San Antonio: University of Texas Institute of Texan Cultures, 1981.

Malsch, Brownson. *Indianola, the Mother of Western Texas.* Abilene: State House Press, 1988.

Monken, Bernard. "Hardships of a German Family." *Frontier Times,* November 1965: 36.

Olmsted, Frederick Law. *Journey Through Texas, A Saddle-Trip on the Southwestern Frontier.* Edited by James Howard. Austin: Von Boeckmann-Jones Press, 1962.

Perry, Garland. *Historic Images of Boerne and Kendall County, Texas.* Boerne: Perry Publications, 1988 and rev. ed. 1998.

Ransleben, Guido E. *A Hundred Years of Comfort In Texas, a Centennial History*. San Antonio: Naylor Co., 1974.

Reinhardt, Louis. "The Communistic Colony of Bettina." *Southwestern Historical Quarterly*, 3: 33 (1899).

Sansom, John W. *The Battle of the Nueces River in Kinney County, Texas, August 10th, 1862*. San Antonio: n.p. 1905.

Sansom, John. Papers. Center for American History, University of Texas at Austin.

Scott, Robert N., ed. *War of the Rebellion: A Compilation of the Official Records of the Union and Confederate Armies*. 128 volumes. Washington, D. C.: Government Printing Office, 1880-1909.

Shook, Robert W. "The Battle of the Nueces, August 10, 1862." *Southwestern Historical Quarterly* 66: 31 (1963).

Smith, Clinton L. *The Boy Captives*. n.p., 1927. Reprint, San Saba: n.p., 2003.

Toepperwein, Lucian Ferdinand. "History of the Family of Ferdinand Lucian Toepperwein." *Toepperwein*. Translated by Flora Wertheim. Boerne: Highland Press, 1984.

Underwood, Rodman L. *Death on the Nueces, German Texans Treue der Union*. Austin: Eakin Press, 2000.

Von Schweinitz, Helga. "Bettina, Communism's Failed Experiment on the Llano," *Old West*, Winter 1992: 52.

Wade, Maria F. *The Native Americans of the Texas Edwards Plateau, 1582-1799*. Austin: University of Texas Press, 2003.

Williams, R. H. *With the Border Ruffians: Memories of the Far West. 1852-1868*. London: J. Murray, 1908.

Image Credits

All images are courtesy of Boerne's Patrick Heath Public Library, except as follows:

Page 10: Author
Page 11: Courtesy of Kendall County Clerk
Page 12: Author
Page 49: UT Institute of Texan Cultures at San Antonio, 068-2449
Page 53: Courtesy of Paul Barwick
Page 56: Author
Page 57: Author
Page 58: Author
Page 59: Author
Page 60: Author
Page 61: Author
Page 62: Author
Page 64: Author
Page 65: Author
Page 66: Author
Page 67: Courtesy of Kenneth Toepperwein
Page 68: Author

www.ingramcontent.com/pod-product-compliance
Lightning Source LLC
LaVergne TN
LVHW051843080426
835512LV00018B/3043